THE WORST-CASE SCENARIO
Survival Guide:
PARANORMAL

THE WORST-CASE SCENARIO
Survival Guide:
PARANORMAL

By David Borgenicht
& Ben H. Winters

Illustrations by Brenda Brown

CHRONICLE BOOKS
SAN FRANCISCO

Copyright © 2011 by Quirk Productions, Inc.

Worst-Case Scenario® and The Worst-Case Scenario Survival Handbook™ are trademarks of Quirk Productions, Inc.

Library of Congress Cataloging-in-Publication Data available.
ISBN: 978-0-8118-7964-4

Manufactured in Canada

Typeset in Adobe Caslon, Bundesbahn Pi, and Zapf Dingbats
Designed by Steven DeCusatis
Illustrations by Brenda Brown

Visit www.worstcasescenarios.com

10 9 8 7 6 5 4 3 2 1

Chronicle Books LLC
680 Second Street
San Francisco, California 94107
www.chroniclebooks.com

WARNING

When a life is imperiled or a dire situation is at hand, safe alternatives may not exist. To deal with the worst-case scenarios presented in this book, we highly recommend—insist, actually—that the best course of action is to consult a professionally trained expert. But because highly trained professionals may not always be available when the safety or sanity of individuals is at risk, we have asked experts on various subjects to describe the techniques they might employ in these emergency situations. THE PUBLISHER, AUTHORS, AND EXPERTS DISCLAIM ANY LIABILITY from any injury that may result from the use, proper or improper, of the information contained in this book. All the answers in this book come from experts in the situation at hand, but we do not guarantee that the information contained herein is complete, safe, or accurate, nor should it be considered a substitute for your good judgment or common sense. Nothing in this book should be construed or interpreted to infringe on the rights of other persons or to violate criminal statutes; we urge you to obey all laws and respect all rights, including property rights, of others.

—The Authors

CONTENTS

Behind every man now alive stands
30 ghosts, for that is the ratio by which
the dead outnumber the living.
—Arthur C. Clarke

I have never met a vampire
personally, but I don't know what
might happen tomorrow.
—Bela Lugosi

INTRODUCTION

As perilous and unpredictable as the normal, physical world can be, when it comes to survival, there's always one thing you can count on: There are rules. The physical world has natural laws that keep it all in check—and that ultimately keep us all alive and well.

Sometimes these are written rules. "Don't feed the bears." "In case of fire, use stairs." Others are unwritten: "What goes up, must come down." "Don't eat something that smells funny." Either way, we all become familiar with such survival basics through good parenting, education, and a bit of trial and error. These rules, along with a calm head and some common sense, help us all make it through everyday life.

But when it comes to the *paranormal* world, things become a bit more challenging. The undead don't operate on the same set of rules as we do—they are much ruder, for one thing. (When was the last time a zombie or vampire knocked?) The laws of science as we understand them today don't always apply in this realm, either. And it's just plain hard to predict how aliens will really behave when they do show up in the skies above Washington, D.C.

But it's safe to say that Stephen Hawking is probably right: When they come, they probably aren't just coming to say hello; they'll be wanting something from us. So you'll need to be prepared—ready to handle things you've never encountered before. Things you don't know the rules about.

That's where this book comes in. *The Worst-Case Scenario Survival Handbook: Paranormal* is the first attempt at publishing an accurate and official collection of the rules for surviving in the realm of the mysterious, the supernatural, the unknown. From performing an exorcism to correctly negotiating with Satan; from fending off a vampire to (safely) breaking up with one; and from breaking a curse to dealing with time paradoxes (the worst!); this manual will provide you with as much information as humanly possible to deal with inhuman perils.

It is our sincere hope that this manual will help you deal with the dangers of the paranormal with the same kind of confidence you have about the dangers of the normal world. So be prepared. Don't panic. Have a plan.

And if you forget your garlic and you don't have a cross or holy water on you, take a look around—there's probably a pizzeria nearby that can help.

—The Authors

CHAPTER 1

THE DEAD AND UNDEAD

HOW TO SLEEP WHEN THE WIND IS MOANING OR SCREAMING

1 Wear yourself out.
Spend the last two hours before bed engaged in vigorous physical activity, such as running up and down a staircase, in terror of whatever dread thing is howling outside.

2 Seek sedation.
Drink cups of chamomile tea or eat a large turkey sandwich and allow their natural sleep-inducing qualities to calm you. Do not think of this as your "last meal."

3 Isolate yourself.
Crawl under the covers wearing noise-canceling headphones and an eye mask to create an isolated sensory environment.

4 Leave the television on.
If it starts to vibrate, change channels by itself, or address you personally by name, turn it off.

5 Generate white noise.
Turn on a loud buzzing fan and noise generating machine in your bedroom. Turn the noise machine to a soothing setting, such as "ocean waves," and turn up the volume all the way.

6 Employ mental exercises.
Select a simple self-calming mantra, like "It's all going to be okay," or "The wind can't hurt you," or "It'll be over quickly." Repeat again and again.

7 | Count sheep.
Tell yourself the horrible moaning is really the sound of fluffy, adorable lambs.

8 | Appease the spirits.
If efforts fail, calm the angry spirits by making whatever sacrifices or offerings they are demanding.

9 | Go mad.
Go quietly insane.

Be Aware
Moaning and howling wind is only rarely encountered on its own. It typically presages a more comprehensive house-haunting experience.

Signs Your House May Be Haunted

Not Haunted	Possibly Haunted	Haunted
Animals not allowed	Animals refuse to enter	Animals spit flame
No hot water	Water sputters	Tap pours ectoplasm
Walls cracked	Walls weep	Walls bleed
Smell of fresh flowers	Smell of rotten milk	Smell of brimstone
Television signal cuts out	Television switches channel itself	Child living in television
Doors creak	Doors slam open and closed	Doors lead to quivering black hellmouth

HOW TO HOST A COCKTAIL PARTY WHEN YOUR HOUSE IS HAUNTED

1 Incorporate haunting into decoration.
Decorate with papier-mâché bats, construction paper ghosts, and bowls of peeled grape "eyeballs." Act as though any unnatural incidents, such as bleeding walls or the appearance of feral cats with gleaming silver eyes, are part of your "haunted" theme.

2 Extend the theme to the food and drink.
Prepare "terrifying" cocktails, such as Zombies and Bloody Marys, and "spooky" hors d'oeuvres, such as ladyfingers and blood sausage.

3 Be confident.
Appear outwardly relaxed and assured to mask your fear and make your guests more comfortable. Treat the haunting like any household inconvenience, offering comments such as "We're working on the problem," and "I know, isn't it a pain? Kind of funny though, right?"

4 Play loud music.
Drown out the sounds of moaning, screaming, and chain rattling with up-tempo hip-hop and/or heavy metal.

5 Steer the conversation.
Minimize the effect of the haunting by bringing up non-paranormal topics for discussion, like work and personal relationships. Encourage friends to argue sensitive issues in order to draw focus away from your "visitors."

6 Play party games.

Announce a drinking game where everyone does a shot each time a door slams by itself. Play "Seven Minutes in the Closet with Whatever the Hell Is in There."

7 Make contact.

If guests persist in being interested in the haunting, go with the flow by organizing a séance or Ouija board session.

8 Sacrifice a partygoer.

Appease the restless spirits with one member of the party. Choose by lots, or pick the person who didn't bring anything.

Decorate with kitschy Halloween housewares to mask signs of actual haunting.

HOW TO PERFORM AN EXORCISM

1 Prepare holy water.
In a clear glass jar that's been sanitized by boiling, collect water from a natural running source such as a stream, waterfall, or rain. Add kosher salt and take to your local priest for a blessing.

2 Dress as if for a rainstorm.
Wear galoshes, a slicker, and a hood.

3 Secure the possessed person.
Tie the victim of demonic control to a bed using strong rope. Bind both hands and feet.

4 Make the sign of the cross over the possessed person.
Repeat every three minutes.

5 Pray for help.
Technically it is God, not you, who will be performing the exorcism. In a clear, commanding voice, intone the liturgy from the Roman Ritual called the Rite of Exorcism, beginning with the Litany of the Saints.

6 Duck.
As you progress through the rite, the demon will cause fluids and viscous material, both human and supernatural, to be expelled violently from its victim.

7 Ignore the demon.
Demons will say hurtful things about you and your family and reveal intimate secrets as a means of psychological evil. Cover your ears and continue the Rite of Exorcism.

Ignore the hurtful things that the demon says about you and your family.

8 | Sprinkle holy water.
Still chanting, splash the blessed water liberally on the possessed person. If it sizzles on their flesh, you know it's working.

9 | Command the demon to exit the person.
Conclude the Rite of Exorcism with the exhortation for the demon to depart, beginning, "Depart, then, impious one, depart."

10 | Unbind the victim.
After the demon has left, free the victim and take him or her for professional medical evaluation.

Be Aware

- A possessed person is sometimes known as a "demoniac."
- The best way to clean up after an exorcism is to have prepared beforehand: Remove breakable or hurlable objects, tape plastic sheeting over walls and floor, and board up windows.
- According to the Catholic Church, only one in about every 5,000 reported cases of demonic possession turns out to be genuine. Individuals seemingly in need of an exorcism may be suffering from a medical condition. Before initiating an exorcism, eliminate the possibility that the victim is suffering from mental illness or seizures.
- Church law dictates that only an ordained priest is allowed to perform an exorcism, and only on orders from his diocesan bishop.
- Exorcised demons frequently take vengeance on the person who expelled them, hounding them for the rest of their lives.

THE RITE OF EXORCISM

The Roman Catholic prayers of exorcism, whether uttered in English or Latin, are extensive—beginning with the Litany of the Saints; continuing with Psalm 53 and readings from the Gospels of John, Mark, and Luke; and ending with the Athanasian Creed. In the middle, however, comes the key exorcism language, which begins as follows. (Note: The crosses in the text indicate where the exorcising priest will make the sign of the cross.)

"I cast you out, unclean spirit, along with every Satanic power of the enemy, every spectre from hell, and all your fell companions; in the name of our Lord Jesus + Christ. Begone and stay far from this creature of God. + For it is He who commands you, He who flung you headlong from the heights of heaven into the depths of hell. It is He who commands you, He who once stilled the sea and the wind and the storm. Hearken, therefore, and tremble in fear, Satan, you enemy of the faith, you foe of the human race, you begetter of death, you robber of life, you corrupter of justice, you root of all evil and vice; seducer of men, betrayer of the nations, instigator of envy, font of avarice, fomentor of discord, author of pain and sorrow. Why, then, do you stand and resist, knowing as you must that Christ the Lord brings your plans to nothing? Fear Him, who in Isaac was offered in sacrifice, in Joseph sold into bondage, slain as the paschal lamb, crucified as man, yet triumphed over the powers of hell. (Note: The three signs of the cross which follow should be traced on the brow of the possessed person.) Begone, then, in the name of the Father, + and of the Son, + and of the Holy + Spirit. Give place to the Holy Spirit by this sign of the holy + cross of our Lord Jesus Christ, who lives and reigns with the Father and the Holy Spirit, one God, forever and ever. Amen."

Signs a Person May Be Possessed
(In Typical Order of Appearance)

- Frightening and confusing dreams
- Appearance of rash, pustules, sores
- Harms self
- Speaks hatefully towards loved ones
- Harms others
- Eyes roll back, fits and convulsions
- Projectile vomiting
- Refuses food and drink
- Spews curses and blasphemies
- Speaks in unfamiliar languages
- Demonstrates knowledge of the secrets of others
- Revulsion to religious objects
- Pained by holy water
- Exhibits superhuman strength
- Levitates spinning in the air
- Announces name of possessing demon or demons

HOW TO CONDUCT A SÉANCE

1 Invite the right people.
Gather a group of six to ten individuals who knew the deceased in life or have some ancestral connection. All attendees should be believers; skeptics are naturally repellent to ghosts.

2 Locate the right spot.
Choose a location with symbolic value to the dead person, such as a favorite room or place of death.

3 Create a comfortable atmosphere.
Begin with a period of relaxed small talk, lasting twenty minutes to half an hour. Choose conversational topics unrelated to death, the deceased, or paranormal communication. Do not serve alcohol.

4 Make a circle.
Seat the group at a small, round table, with enough room so everyone can sit close but without touching knees.

5 Create a welcoming environment for the spirit.
Turn down the lights. Put on classical piano music and light candles scented with sandalwood and patchouli, unless you know the deceased hated such things, in which case improvise according to taste.

6 Invoke your purpose.
Softly chant the name of the deceased, inviting him to join you. In gentle but commanding tones, say, "Spirit we summon you, join us now. Spirit we summon you, join us now." Instruct the others to join in your chant.

7 Be brave.

Spirits are discouraged by fear. As you chant, remind yourself that spirits have no power over those who invoke them.

8 Greet the spirit.

You will become aware of the presence of the deceased inside you. Stop chanting and remain perfectly quiet, allowing the voice of the deceased to speak in your mind. Think questions you would like answered by the departed.

9 Reveal what has been communicated.

After fifteen to twenty minutes of reflective listening, break the silence and go clockwise around the room, asking each person to reveal what the spirit said to them. Not all of them will have heard from the spirit— assure them that this is normal and discourage them from faking contact in order to "fit in."

Be Aware

- The popular image of the séance, with the levitating table and ghost appearing in the corner of the room, is a Hollywood invention.
- It may take several sessions before you are successful in conjuring the spirit of the dead.

How to Get the Dead to Leave You Alone

1 Be firm.
Once a ghost is aware that it can reach you, it may not have a good sense of personal boundaries and will try to talk your ear off. When the ghost appears, use a firm, calm voice (both inner and audible) to compel it to depart. Be consistent; even if the ghost returns in a more appealing form, repeat your desire for it to stop talking to you.

2 Block inner channels.
If you have been hosting séances or other reaching-out activities, cease them immediately. Imagine a happy, soothing "place of peace" and think of it anytime thoughts of death or spirits begin to well up in your mind.

3 Stay busy.
Ghosts in search of human connection may glom onto those with excessive spare time. Spend more time at work and develop a more active social life.

4 Move.
Many ghosts are moored to a particular location. Relocate to a new place, ensuring first that it is not built over the site of an old burial ground or abandoned mental hospital.

5 Satisfy their requests.
Perform whatever action the ghost is asking you specifically to do, such as returning the gold you stole and thought no one knew about or reburying his improperly interred body.

MEANS OF COMMUNICATING WITH THE DEAD

Means of Communication	The Basics	Pros	Cons
Séance	Small group chants in dark, invites the dead	Dramatic	May take many tries to work
Ouija board	Board game contacts the other side	Fun for parties	May accidentally invite demons
Waking dream	Spirit met in supernatural desert of the soul	Subject feels like rock star or guru	Subject always wakes up before the really good part
Hire a medium	Professional dead-whisperer delivers your message	Can hand off messy personal issues	Medium gets all the credit if things go well
Channeling	Invite dead person to take over your body	Extremely intimate	Will they ever leave?
Visiting the underworld	Journey to Hell in company of Virgil	Can ask the damned anything you want	May get extremely hot
Skype	Internet video link	Picture-in-picture spiritual communication	Service spotty in lowest levels of Hell

HOW TO PHOTOGRAPH A GHOST

1 Control the lighting.

Light cast from multiple sources will make it difficult to determine which effects are optical and which are supernatural. If the haunted location is indoors, control the sources of lighting by closing doors, shutting curtains, and reducing the number of interior lights that are on so that it is clear what light is, or isn't, coming from the expected sources in the room. For outdoor locations, avoid taking photographs facing into or at a 90-degree angle from the sun or a bright moon, as this may cause lens flare. Attach a lens hood to your camera.

2 Bring an assistant/witness.

Ask one or more other people to accompany you to help watch for paranormal activity at the site, and to serve as additional witnesses once it occurs. Give each a camera to help document the event.

3 Bring audio and video recorders.

Set up audio and video recorders at the haunted site to further document what transpires and provide corroborating evidence to your photography. Leave them running at all times to capture unexpected events.

4 Use film cameras.

Though digital pictures allow you to see the image immediately, the use of traditional film provides you with both the negative and the final print to refer to. Also, not only are digital images easier to deliberately tamper with, they are also more prone to natural optical artifacts that can be mistaken for ghosts, raising the possibility that your work will be dismissed by skeptics. Set the cameras to the fastest rapid

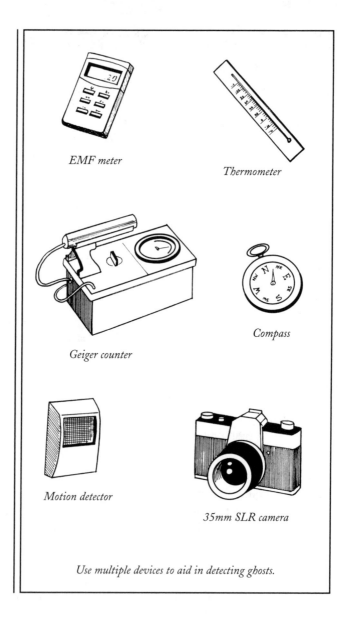

EMF meter

Thermometer

Geiger counter

Compass

Motion detector

35mm SLR camera

Use multiple devices to aid in detecting ghosts.

frame or multi-burst setting it allows—this will provide you with as many images as possible of a fleeting event.

5 | Use detection devices.
Strong, rapid fluctuations in the readings of any of these devices, and especially of several of them at once, can indicate the presence of a ghost: EMF meters, thermometers, compasses, Geiger counters, and infrared motion detectors.

6 | Wait.
The ghost may be leery of your presence and not appear right away. Get comfortable, and bring food and provisions to last for a full day or more of watchful waiting.

7 | At the first sign of weirdness, begin shooting.
Ghosts do not always emerge in human form; be on alert for slow floating mist, a cloud of ectoplasm or vapor, an orb or a swirling ball of light, and muttering voices from no clear source.

8 | Shoot plentifully.
Don't hesitate to wonder whether you should take another photo: you always should. Remain at the site and continue photographing even after the visible duration of the event to allow for the possibility of the film capturing after-effects not visible to the naked eye.

Be Aware
- Many famous ghost pictures have been captured by accident, when vacationers or other casual photographers discovered paranormal beings on developed film.
- Some ghost photographers shoot with infrared film, which can reveal details not visible on regular film.

HOW TO GET RID OF A GHOST

1 Assemble and outfit a team.

Gather a number of people who share your belief in the paranormal and your desire to rid the haunted space of its ghostly inhabitant. Each ghost hunter should carry a walkie-talkie or cell phone, a digital recording device, a compass, a thermometer, and a flashlight with spare batteries. The group should also carry among them a thermal imaging camera, portable ion generator, electromagnetic field meter, Geiger counter, infrared motion detector, and a laser grid.

2 Prepare psychologically and spiritually.

Join hands and pray for protection and power against the ghost. Anyone harboring any skepticism regarding the existence of the ghost should be expelled from the group.

3 Activate the ion generator.

A portable ion generator creates a large cloud of electric activity. Sudden disruptions or increases in the intensity of the cloud can indicate the presence of a spirit.

4 Deploy the simple detection devices.

Hold the compass and the thermometer outstretched in front of you as you move through the space. The compass needle will swing away from true north in the presence of a ghost; the readings of the thermometer will spike or dip.

5 Deploy the higher-functioning detection devices.

If there are enough members of your party, give each one of the devices and move independently, sweeping the area. Use the electromagnetic field meter to register bursts of electrical activity; the Geiger counter to measure changes in radiation level; the laser grid for the detection of shadow masses; and the handheld infrared motion detector to read movement invisible to the eye.

6 Traverse the haunted area.
Walk in slow, methodical steps covering all parts of the haunted area with each detection device, shining flashlights and ultraviolet headlamps into all dark corners. Your goal is twofold: to become comfortable with the environment, and to allow the ghosts or spirits to become comfortable with your presence.

7 Remain in contact.
If group members are not in visual contact with one another, establish a schedule of contact for checking in with one another depending on your knowledge of the disposition of the ghost. If you have reason to believe the ghost is angry or hostile, allow no more than five minutes between contact.

8 Watch for anomalies.
Pay attention to your detection equipment for strange readings or rapid gyrations. Abrupt changes in climate or weather, such as sudden lightning, thunder, heavy rain, fast-moving fog, or sinkholes may foretell the appearance of a ghost—particularly if these events occur indoors.

9 Counsel the ghost.
When the ghost appears, acknowledge its existence, and gently explain to it that it is dead, and has become a ghost. Ask the ghost if it wants to tell or show you something, after which it may be free to depart. Most ghosts are not malevolent, but rather the restless, unmoored spirits of tragedy victims. A show of empathy is often enough to dematerialize the ghost and grant it freedom from our plane of existence.

10 Command the ghost to depart.

If the ghost does not respond to empathy, command it to leave in a forceful, clear voice, telling it to begone in the name of holy spirits more powerful than itself, according to your beliefs. Repeat the order, and have all members of your group do the same, until the ghost leaves.

11 "Smudge" the ghost.

If the ghost remains, light a small bundle of sage and walk through the haunted area, letting the smoke blow freely to fill the air and all corners of any indoor space until the sage burns down. As you walk, allow the ashes to scatter and chant the words, "This place is cleansed of spirits. In God's holy name, this place is free."

12 Protect yourself.

Invoke the protection of pure holy spirits to ensure that no other malevolent spirits come to re-inhabit this space, or to follow you from it.

Be Aware

- Commonly haunted places include buildings situated on or near graveyards and battlefields; hotels and motels; theaters; former mental hospitals or orphanages; and otherwise seemingly normal suburban homes.
- Types of ghosts you may find include a dead human, who for whatever reason is not ready to go to the other side; or a nonhuman spirit, which is generally much more likely to be aggressive.

HOW TO CLEAN A WALL DRIPPING WITH BLOOD

1 Write down the message.

Before you begin cleaning, write down any messages written in the blood. Transcribe the message in its entirety, even if it seems really easy to remember ("Get out"). If the message seems nonsensical ("REDRUM"), hold a mirror up to it and read the reflection.

2 Wet the wall thoroughly with a detergent solution.

Mix one-quarter ounce of concentrated medical enzyme detergent in a gallon of hot water. Using a wet mop with a wide mouth, slowly cover the entire wall, moving in rows from top to bottom.

3 Home in on the worst areas.

Attack heavily bloodied areas with a wadded rag dipped in the detergent solution; repeat.

4 Clean and clean and clean.

Clean furiously, cursing this damned house, until your muscles ache and beads of sweat gather on your brow.

5 Repaint the wall.

Use a dark color, such as maroon or scarlet, against which future blood eruptions will be less visible.

6 Pause for new blood.

If the wall begins bleeding anew while you are painting, wait until it stops before continuing to paint. Repeat steps one to three, if necessary, before resuming.

7 Stock up on paint.

In a profoundly haunted house, a bleeding wall will frequently bleed again as soon as you have repainted it. Be prepared to paint again the following day, and then again and again.

8 Try alternate coverage.

Wallpaper adds an added layer of material coverage but is much more difficult to replace in the event of bleed-through. Tiling will allow the blood to seep between the cracks, but it may be able to be spot-cleaned with a damp cloth or sponge.

Be Aware

- The walls most likely to bleed are interior walls, non-windowed walls, old walls (from the original structure, if the house has been extensively renovated), or those entombing the dead.
- Before removing a wall entirely, check with an architect that it is not a load-bearing bleeding wall.

HOW TO TELL IF YOU'RE DEAD

It is a rare but not unheard-of phenomenon that a person will die and become a ghost while remaining unaware of this change in status.

⭐ **The "grammar check."**
When people speak about you, note whether they do so in the present or past tense.

⭐ **The "appropriateness check."**
Listen for the sorts of statements people avoid in the presence of a living person, such as "I never told her I loved her" or "I never liked that guy."

⭐ **The "interaction check."**
Note whether other individuals respond when you speak directly to them. Eliminate other reasons for ignoring you, such as inappropriate behavior or poor hygiene.

⭐ **Consult an expert.**
Find someone who speaks to dead people professionally, such as a medium or creepy psychic child, and ask them whether you are a ghost.

⭐ **Judge your ability to have physical affect.**
You may be able to lift and hold certain objects, but these may be spirit-objects that only you can see. Try performing an action with the object, such as hitting a baseball or another person.

⭐ **The "fork check."**
Poke yourself in the forearm with a fork, the point of a pencil, or other sharp object. Does it hurt?

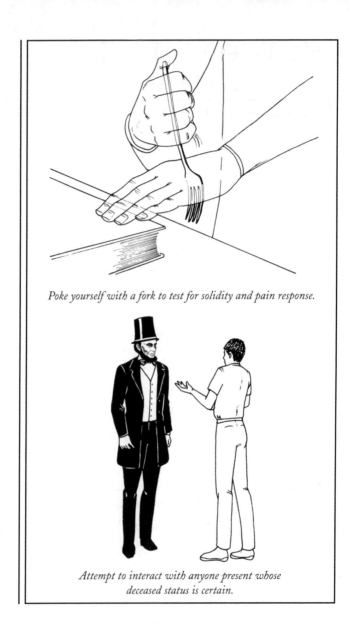

Poke yourself with a fork to test for solidity and pain response.

Attempt to interact with anyone present whose deceased status is certain.

✪ Attempt to fly.
Squeeze your eyes shut tightly and imagine yourself soaring across the air, ducking in and out of moonbeams. Open your eyes and note whether or not you are actually doing so.

✪ Try to speak to other dead people.
Speak to people who you know have passed away and see if you receive a response.

✪ Look at yourself in the mirror.
Are you there?

Be Aware
• Having a conversation with a seemingly living person does not always mean you are alive; it is possible the speaker is also dead, and neither one of you is aware of it.

DISTINGUISHING A FRIENDLY GHOST FROM AN UNFRIENDLY GHOST

Trait	Friendly	Unfriendly
Name	Casper	Creepy Jimmy
Appearance	All-white with googly eyes	Gnarled or disfigured corpse
Says	"Boo"	[terrifying shriek]
Advanced display of powers	Slides down the stairs in old-timey hat, singing "It's Later Than You Think"	Causes your walls to buckle, weep; throws you down the stairs
Relationship with children	Helps them play gentle pranks	Lures them to the well

HOW TO REANIMATE A MUMMY

1   Find the right mummy.

Many mummies are pharaohs or members of a pharaoh's entourage. Others are merely criminals who were mummified alive as punishment. Find a mummy whose tongue has been cut out, but who is otherwise undamaged, and whose tomb is filled with the fossilized remnants of scarab beetles.

2   Search for curses.

As you descend the stairway, proceed through the long, sloped corridor, cross the "handing-over room," and enter the burial chamber. Shine your flashlight along the floor and the lintels of the doorways, looking for inscriptions.

3   Record the curses.

Transcribe the hieroglyphs in a waterproof notebook to fully understand and avoid whatever fate might await you for the crime against nature that you are about to commit.

4   Pry open the sarcophagus.

Enter the burial chamber and use a crowbar to force open the heavy, human-shaped lid sealing the mummy inside the coffin.

5   Brace yourself.

Adapt a wide stance, planting your feet firmly on the floor to prepare for the waves of eerie power that will emanate from the mummy when its soul is reunited with its flesh.

6 Invoke the Egyptian god Thoth.

Read aloud the central passage from the Scroll of Thoth: "Oh God of Gods! Death is but the doorway to new life! We live today, and we shall live again! In many and various forms shall we return, oh Mighty One!"

7 Repeat.

As the mummy begins to stir, continue to recite the passage from the Scroll of Thoth, increasing in volume to assert your power over the revived corpse.

8 Reunite the deceased with its *ren*.

As the power of Thoth brings the corpse to life and he staggers forth from his sarcophagus, chant the name of the deceased over and over. Egyptian lore holds that a person's *ren*, or name, was a part of his soul, stripped at the moment of death, which must be restored at the moment of reanimation.

9 Perform the Opening of the Mouth ceremony.

Hold a calf's leg up to the mouth of the mummy and anoint the shoulders with a metal-plated adze (hand-shaped wand) while chanting the relevant text from plates V and VI of the Book of the Dead: "My mouth is opened by Ptah / My mouth's bonds are loosed by my city-god / Thoth has come fully equipped with spells / He looses the bonds of Seth from my mouth / Atum has given me my hands / They are placed as guardians."

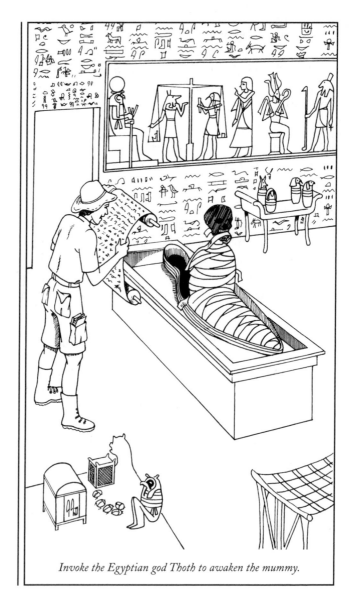

Invoke the Egyptian god Thoth to awaken the mummy.

10 | Pass back through the handing-over room.

Lead the mummy back through the antechamber that separates the burial chamber from the stairs. By guiding him back through the place where his corpse was symbolically handed over to death, you are assuming power over him in his reanimated life.

11 | Do your malevolent will.

Guide the hideous, desiccated creature into the world of the living, and bid him wreak havoc upon your adversaries.

Be Aware

- Some tombs contain more than one mummy. In the Valley of the Golden Mummies, 106 tombs were found together housing thousands of mummies, including one entire extended family of 42 people.

- The tombs of some mummies are cursed in such a way that, upon an intruder's entrance, the mummy reanimates automatically. The first act of such mummies is always to attack the intruder.

- In Egyptian spirituality, the five parts of the soul are the *ka*, *ba*, *ib*, *sheut*, and *ren*, translating roughly as "spirit," "soul," "heart," "shadow," and "name."

- The book of funerary rites commonly known in Western culture as the Book of the Dead is actually titled *Spells of Coming Forth by Day*. Text from this book, often inscribed in black resin on papyrus, can almost always be found somewhere in the sarcophagus, where it was placed by priests to guide the deceased in negotiating the afterlife.

HOW TO SURVIVE A MUMMY'S CURSE

1 Find the curse.

On entering the pharaoh's tomb, look to the lintels of the doorway or on the walls for the curse inscribed there. Translate from the hieroglyphics, watching for word forms such as "eternal suffering" and "unto the seventh generation."

2 Record the curse.

Copy the text of the curse into your notebook, underlining unfamiliar hieroglyphics for later translation.

3 Minimize corpse contact.

Pharaohs are far more likely to enact curses on those who defile their physical bodies.

4 Keep your hands to yourself.

Leave the dozens upon dozens of precious items in the treasure room, located behind the burial chamber, exactly as you found them. Do not remove from the tomb— or even touch—any of the jewels, household objects, inscribed scarabs, mummified cats, masks, combs and brushes, mirrors, furniture, pictures, papyruses, trumpets, board games, statues, daggers, fans, sandals, or other items that you find.

5 Pray for forgiveness.

Immediately upon exiting the tomb, direct a prayer to the ever-lasting *ba*, or soul, of the deceased, thanking it for hosting you in the tomb.

6 | Keep mum.
Publicizing your discovery not only risks another adventurer stealing the treasure but will also enrage the spirit of the pharaoh.

7 | Refer to the inscribed curses.
Once home, refer to your notebook for the specific dangers that may await you, as per the warnings you copied from the tomb walls. If necessary, take your notebook to an Egyptologist for translation.

8 | Don't eat fish.
A set of curses directed at the priests who performed the rite of mummification instructs them to abstain from fish. Contemporary mummy experts advise tomb raiders to do likewise.

9 | Avoid the southern hemisphere.
Mosquito bites are a notorious source of death for cursed tomb raiders. Avoid tropical climates and wear long sleeves and pants at all times. Sleep under a mosquito net.

10 | Be careful around blades.
Lord Carnavon, discoverer of Tut's tomb in the Valley of Kings, died of a mysterious infection after a simple razor cut. Avoid razors, fingernail clippers, knives, and any other sharp objects for a period beginning after you disturb the mummy and lasting until you die of natural causes.

11 Keep an eye on your friends and animals.

Howard Carter, who accompanied Lord Carnavon, did not himself die from the Curse of the Mummy; however, his pet canary was eaten by a snake.

12 Undo the curse.

Break into the tomb again and destroy the mummy by tearing out its heart and burning it.

Be Aware

- The tombs of pharaohs or other powerful personages, such as spell casters and priests, are the most likely to be cursed, although regular people, if wealthy, would also curse their tombs to prevent the plunder of goods.

- Failure in Step 12 may result in a renewed and more wrathful curse.

HOW TO KILL
A MUMMY

1 Steal its tana leaves.

Mummies are sometimes buried clutching a handful of this mystical flora to keep their hearts beating, and they will cling to them after being reanimated.

2 Tear off and destroy the amulet.

Remove the glowing ruby-red amulet from around the mummy's neck, along with any other jewelry the creature bears, and smash it with a hammer.

3 Light the mummy on fire.

Mummies were typically preserved in highly flammable materials such as linen and soaked in flammable resins, so they are extremely susceptible to burning. Toss a torch at the pursuing mummy.

4 Tear out the heart.

Once the mummy has burned down to a blackened skeleton, crack open its rib cage with a shovel or the claw of a hammer and remove the heart.

5 Burn the heart.

Douse the shriveled organ in lighter fluid and set it ablaze.

6 Scatter the ashes in the desert sand.

Gather up the ashes of the mummy, the heart, and the shattered pieces of the amulet and other jewelry, and let them be loosed upon the desert winds, never again to be reunited.

7 Blot out the unholy name.

Gather up any scrolls or papyruses that mention the mummified person and destroy them. Smash statues, burn drawings, and dispose of any other iconography relating to him to ensure that his soul is forever annihilated.

Be Aware

- Some mummies were mummified without hearts, but instead with a stone icon of a scarab beetle left in the chest in its place. If that is the case, crush the stone with a hammer.
- A mummy cannot be injured by guns or knives; in addition, if the mummified person had supernatural powers in life, such as the ability to cast spells, he will retain those powers as a mummy.
- Like zombies, reanimated mummies tend to be interested in murdering the living. However, some mummies may fall in love with the beautiful daughters of Egyptologists or archaeologists, especially if the daughter bears a striking resemblance to the woman the mummy loved in life.

HOW TO KILL
A VAMPIRE

1 Seek the grave.
Use a white wolf, or a dog with "four eyes" (having eye-shaped marks above or below the eyes), to sniff out a vampire's grave among regular human graves.

2 Look for balls of light.
Confirm that it is a vampire's grave by spotting bright balls of weird blue-white light that may be floating over the site; these represent an alternate, ethereal form that some vampires can take, rather than remaining in their fleshy bodies.

3 Apply garlic, ashes, and salt.
When you have identified the grave of a vampire, neutralize the monster's power by sowing the ground with salt and ash. Reinforce this protection by wearing a clove of garlic around your neck.

4 Open the grave.
If you are dealing with a not-yet-risen vampire, the coffin may still be buried in a graveyard. If the vampire is already experienced in the afterlife, its coffin will likely be above ground in a mausoleum, castle, or other location. Dig up the coffin if necessary, using a pointed spade or modern excavation equipment, if available. Pry the coffin open with a crowbar.

5 Double-check.

Be sure it is a vampire by holding a mirror up to it (vampires will cast no reflection) noting whether blood is dripping from the corners of its mouth and whether the color of its flesh is flushed and vital. If it is *not* a vampire, reinter the corpse.

6 Drive a stake through the heart and the skull.

Using the flat of your shovel as a cudgel, drive a wooden stake through the vampire's heart and another through its mouth into its skull.

7 Chop up the body.

Hack the body to pieces to ensure that no further revivification is possible. Swords, farming implements, and power tools are all effective.

8 Burn the body parts.

To prevent any corpse-stealing monster builders from acquiring vampire parts, build a ritual pyre and throw the pieces of the vampire on it, adding the clothing, personal effects, and anything else found inside the monster's grave.

9 Scatter the ashes in a swift-moving river.

Be Aware

- Anyone who comes into contact with the blood of a vampire while trying to kill it risks going mad and/or becoming a vampire.
- If the staking does not work, the vampire may rise up, draw out the stake, and use it to strike at the living.

*Use a white wolf or a dog with "four eyes" markings
to sniff out the vampire's grave.*

How to Fend Off a Vampire if You Don't Have Garlic

⭐ Douse the vampire with holy water.

⭐ Confront with a cross.
Some vampires are merely repulsed by the sight of crosses and other Christian iconography; less powerful vampires or those more recently created can be destroyed by them. True Christian crucifixes are preferable to makeshift crosses.

⭐ Seek sunlight.
If you are struggling with a vampire and dawn is breaking, flee outside.

⭐ Create a false daybreak.
Vampires can be fooled into thinking day has begun if they hear sounds associated with morning, such as a crowing rooster or the ringing of a church's *matin* bells.

⭐ Use peppermint.
Many vampires are repelled by this herb's strong smell and taste.

⭐ Wave onions.
Though less effective than garlic, other soil-grown vegetables such as onions and shallots may also work.

⭐ Hang a net across the door.
Certain cursed vampires, when confronted with a net, are compelled to count all its holes.

⭐ Spill grains of white rice.
Similarly, some vampires will be supernaturally compelled to halt their pursuit and count every grain of rice.

Be Aware

Vampire vulnerabilities vary from region to region and even from vampire to vampire, depending on where or how they were turned. No one repellent, including garlic, is guaranteed to work.

How Much Blood Is in a . . .

Creature	Pints of Blood	Tasting Notes
Human (150 pounds)	10	Coppery, salty
Dog (30 pounds)	2	Full bodied
Rabbit (10 pounds)	0.66	Gamey
Cat (10 pounds)	0.66	Floral notes
Monkey (60 pounds)	4	Subtle finish
Pig (200 pounds)	13	Full bodied, earthy
Bat (2 pounds)	0.13	Mysterious, piquant
Chicken (6 pounds)	0.4	Tastes like chicken

HOW TO DATE A VAMPIRE IF YOU ARE A "MORNING PERSON"

★ Let him sleep.
Depending on what strain of vampirism your partner is cursed with, sunlight may be unpleasant, harmful, or outright fatal to him, and thus his life is likely oriented around the nighttime hours. When you are ready to wake up and start the day, your vampire will still be sleeping off a long night of bloodfeast. Go for a solitary jog or curl up with the paper until he's ready to arise.

★ Be respectful.
Don't perform loud activities, such as vacuuming (which can wake a vampire) or ringing church bells (which can destroy one).

★ Demand respect in return.
If his entry and exit from his coffin are loud and disrupt your sleep, ask for consideration as he moves about in the dead of night.

★ Sleep separately.
Intimate relationships do not necessarily require sleeping in the same bed. You take the cozy bedroom; he has his coffin filled with cemetery dirt in the basement.

Be aware of loud activities that could disrupt a vampire's sleep.

57. *how to date a vampire if you are a "morning person"*

★ Experiment.
Explore your mutual interest in vampires through daylight-safe indoor activities such as hosting your own vampire film festival, comparing and discussing the creatures' depiction in various movies and TV shows. What did they get right? What did they get wrong?

★ Find mutually agreeable times for togetherness.
Go for walks together in the last purple hour of daylight, when the sun is slowly sinking, before you get too tired and he is compelled to feed.

★ Communicate with notes.
Slip an affectionate message, such as "I love you—happy hunting!" into the fold of his cape to remind him even when he's at work that you're thinking of him.

★ Reorient your sleep schedule.
The human circadian rhythm can be retrained to sleep during the day and wake at night; consider changing your habits to match those of your vampire partner. The key is regularity: Stay up all night the first time, go to sleep at dawn in a dark room, and make yourself stick to that pattern, resisting the impulse to get out of bed during midday, until it feels natural to wake fresh in the early evening every day.

★ Use his powers.
Many vampires have the ability to appear in dreams. Ask your vampire to visit you in your dreams.

HOW TO SURVIVE A LOVE TRIANGLE WITH A WEREWOLF AND A VAMPIRE

1 Juggle.
Use a calendar to block off the best times to be with each creature according to its own infernal cycles. Plan dates with the werewolf for nights with a waning moon so that he's not preoccupied with the physical challenges of transformation; with the vampire, schedule together time on nights with a fuller moon and for just after he has recently feasted, when he will be sated and more ready to engage in other activities.

2 Take your time.
Both partners enjoy eternal life, so don't feel rushed to make up your mind for their sakes.

3 Be honest.
When either relationship becomes serious, inform each creature that you are involved with the other and make clear the priority in which you hold the relationship.

4 Avoid scenes.
Both werewolves and vampires possess ferocious animal instincts and are quick to anger. Try not to let them encounter the other, especially in your presence.

5 Find a nice human boy.
Break up with both monsters. Move to a new town and pray for your own safety and that of your new beau.

Plan your calendar to avoid crossing the nocturnal schedules
of your vampire and werewolf companions.

HOW TO BREAK UP WITH A VAMPIRE

1 Brood dramatically.
Pace the floors of the castle. Stare up at the cold light of the moon. Sigh, moan, and curse the day you ever met him.

2 Weigh the pros and cons.
Confirm that you have made the right decision by making a list of plusses and minuses to continuing the relationship. List as many cons (e.g., committed to evil) as possible. For any pros (e.g., promise of eternal life), are there downsides (e.g., eternal boredom)?

3 Pick a good time.
Don't break up with the vampire on Valentine's Day, his birthday or rebirth day, or when he hasn't feasted for several days.

4 Look away.
It can be hard to maintain your nerve while staring into the literally mesmerizing eyes of a vampire. Close your eyes, or look out the window, while telling him how you feel.

5 Be brief and direct.
As with any breakup, your goal is to tell the truth without being overly informative. Say your piece and then stop speaking.

6 Don't make it about the vampirism.
Find other reasons to explain the breakup, such as his personal habits or friends, rather than the fact that he is a heartless, shape-shifting destroyer of men.

7 Be firm.
The vampire may protest, saying that he can change. Remind yourself that he's been alive for many centuries and genuine change is unlikely.

8 Keep it about the two of you.
If you have fallen for someone else, do not mention it; vampires are notorious seekers of vengeance.

9 Skip the goodbye kiss.

How to Get Over a Vampire

⭐ Give yourself time.
A good rule of thumb is that getting over someone takes half the length of time as the relationship itself. If you've been dating the vampire for countless millennia, count on a similarly epic grieving period.

⭐ Remove evidence of the vampire from your life.
Don't listen to his favorite songs; throw away his old capes; scrub the bloodstains from around the house.

⭐ Focus on the bad times.
When you think of the vampire, remember the tedious nights spent traipsing through graveyards, the gross spectacle of his feasting on human flesh, and how cold and distant he could be.

⭐ Find someone new.
Avoid dating other vampires, since you will be more likely to run into your ex at social events. Consider dating in another species or professional circle, such as a werewolf or a warlock.

Shapes Assumed by Vampires

Shape	Frequency	How to Tell It's a Vampire
Cat	Very frequent	Hisses at all humans, forked tongue
Dog	Rare	Eats bones, glowing eyes
Bat	Frequent	Flies alone, sleeps with eyes open
Fog or mist	Very frequent	Exceptionally cold, moves with clear intention
Wolf	Frequent	Walks upright; cold, human eyes
Insect	Rare	Leaps or flies further than normal insect
Bird	Extremely rare	Blood dripping from beak
Attractive human woman (succubus)	Rare	Nymphomaniacal, fanged
Debonair human man	Frequent	Silk cape, fangs, Eastern European accent

VAMPIRES OF THE WORLD

Name	Tradition	Appearance	Special Qualities
Nuckelavee	Scottish	Skinless, half human, half horse	Kills with bad breath
Yuki-onna	Japanese	Beautiful lady in white	Blood-drinking fog-breather
Eretik	Russian	Dead heretic turned cannibal vampire	Killable with fire or aspen stake
the rakshasas	Hindu	Night demons	Infant killers
Varkolak	Eastern European	40-days-dead outlaw-turned-monster	Stores flesh of victims in cave
Dhampir	Balkan	Soft body, untamed dark hair, may lack a shadow	Product of vampire mother, human father; extremely powerful
loogaroo	Caribbean	Skinless	Hides in tree, shoots flame from bodily orifices
chiang-shih	Chinese	Reanimated corpse with claws, fangs	Blind; must track victims by their breathing
Camazotz	Mayan	Half bat, half man	Soul-eating cave god
the yara-ma-yha-who	Australian Aborigine	Little red man with a big head and mouth	Eats people, regurgitates them, eats them again
alp	German	Little elf vampire	Sits on chests of women, sucks blood through breasts
Penanggalan	Malaysian	Flying detached head with dangling entrails	Eats babies
Count Chocula	General Mills	Grinning, brown-caped	Delicious chocolate marshmallow bits

HOW TO ADJUST TO BECOMING A VAMPIRE

1 | Mourn.
Grieve your departed mortal self, now forever banished. Reread old letters, drive by your old high school, call old girlfriends, and relive happier, more human times.

2 | Separate.
Break the bond with the vampire who created you, either through violent combat or with a polite e-mail.

3 | Cut off contact with your mortal friends.
It will be difficult for you and your loved ones to adjust to your new undead status. Consider moving to a new town where people don't know you and you can feel free to "be yourself."

4 | Location, location, location.
Stake out your own territory, away from other vampires, where you won't encroach on the stalking ground of others.

5 | Practice on animals.
Satiate your bloodlust first on small animals and work your way up in victim size until you feel comfortable trying a person.

6 | Create your first victim.
You will not truly be a vampire until you have tasted human blood and made someone else a vampire. Popular nocturnal hunting grounds include bars and nightclubs. Although the crowds in these places are plentiful and easy, take your time, and choose a victim you won't mind having around for all eternity.

Make full use of the vampire's traditional wardrobe.

7 | Learn to enjoy the taste of blood.
Though you are compelled by unholy need to drink blood, this does not mean you will necessarily enjoy the taste. Experiment with different kinds (the blood of the young, old, men or women) until you find a flavor that's right for you.

8 | Dress the part.
Inhabit your new self more fully by acquiring and wearing various vampire accoutrements, such as a long silk cape and pointy black shoes.

9 | Experiment with forms.
Each night, turn yourself into something different—fog, a bat, a wolf—until you feel comfortable maneuvering in each guise.

10 | Get a hobby.
Experiencing eternity can be extremely tedious. Learn to play chess, do needlepoint, solve sudoku puzzles, and foster your interest in other engaging activities.

11 | Hire a sidekick.
Many successful vampires employ a hunchback or madman to provide assistance and company. If none are immediately available, try an online classified ad or job sites such as Craigslist or Monster.com.

12 | Terrorize your neighborhood.
When you feel comfortable, begin terrorizing the local populace. They may be angry at first, but soon they will come to know and fear you.

Be Aware

Once you have become a vampire, the only way to reverse the curse is to be destroyed by a vampire hunter.

What to Expect if You've Been Bitten

Right away: Severe pain at bite site, bloody discharge from and around wound.

Within one week: Continuing severe pain, accompanied by weakness. Fang marks do not fade and may even become redder and more vivid. Severe pain around wound site.

Within two to three weeks: Disruption of sleeping patterns (nocturnal insomnia, lethargy during the day). Sensitivity to sunlight develops; increased intake of red meat and iron.

Within one month: Canine teeth sharpen and extend. Increased tolerance for pain.

Within three months: Ability to transform into fog, smoke, and mist.

The remainder of eternity: Revulsion for religious artifacts, imperviousness to mortal pain, hatred for the living, insatiable desire to feed on the blood and souls of humans.

Be Aware
Depending on the strain of vampirism involved, this time line may be greatly accelerated.

Various Demons

Name	Governs	Tradition
Aeshma	Wrath and rage	Zoroastrian
Akop	Widowed people	Filipino
Alrinach	Shipwrecks	Christian
Anamalech	Bad news	Assyrian
Ascaroth	Spies	Christian
Antaura	Migraine headaches	Greek
Azi	Greed	Zoroastrian
Bar egra	Going to work	Syrian
Belphegor	Sexual prowess, penises	Hebrew & Christian
Busyasta	Sleeping in	Zoroastrian
Daitya	Oceans	Hindu
Hel	The dead	Norse
Hemah	Death of domestic animals	Hebrew
Itzpapalotl	Witches	Aztec
Kasha	Corpses	Japanese
Kunda	Drunkenness	Zoroastrian
Leshy	Wild animals, forests	Slavic
Naamah	Prostitution	Hebrew
Pazuzu	Diseases, plagues	Assyrian
Rahu	Eclipses	Hindu
Saalah	The woods	Christian
Spenjargak	Storms	Buddhist
Taru	Hunger	Zoroastrian
Ukobach	Fireworks, fried food	Christian
Xic	Sudden death	Guatemalan

HOW TO SEND A DEMON BACK TO HELL

⭐ Invoke a more powerful spirit.
Most demons are craven, low-level spirits who will tremble at the name or image of the Taoist deity Shoki (known as the "demon queller") or the archangel Michael. Brandish a picture or icon and chant the name of the more powerful spirit.

⭐ Ring bells.
Ancient Assyrian magical tradition and Christian theologies cite bells as a means of driving off evil spirits. Bells should always be rung during storms, which represent the presence of demons in the air.

⭐ Fling salt at the demon.
Salt, particularly sea salt, represents the divine purity of the ocean, which gods of several traditions use to wash away evil.

⭐ Wear an amulet.
Most spiritual traditions employ protective devices such as amulets to ward off evil spirits; most demons cannot stand the sight of such items. Put on the Jewish tefillin, hang a Hindu talisman around your neck, wave the Christian cross, and brandish crystals.

⭐ Chant.
Employ a simple Gregorian chant or rhythmically recite "Ave Maria."

Escalate demon-banishing practices as necessary: ringing a bell, flinging salt, wearing an amulet, drawing a magic circle.

⭐ Burn the liver of a fish.
As the Archangel Raphael demonstrates in the biblical book of Tobit, the fumes of burnt fish liver drive off evil spirits.

⭐ Lose the demon in winding paths.
Low-level demons are capable of traveling only in straight lines and become baffled along a winding path, where they can then be trapped and banished.

⭐ Paint the ceiling.
Coat the ceiling of your home with sky blue to trick a house-haunting demon into ascending to celestial realms.

⭐ Trap the demon in a magic circle.
Draw a nine-foot circle on the ground and then draw a seven-pointed pentacle inside; consult a copy of the Key of Solomon for the appropriate incantation to catch and subdue the demon within. After the demon disappears, burn the ground where you had etched the circle.

Be Aware
- The word *demon* refers to a wide variety of spirits, devils, and fallen angels.
- Demons do not always appear in a tangible or visible form. Signs of demonic presence include extremely vivid nightmares, a strange absence of light in your home, or a mysterious bad smell.
- Like bears, demons smell fear and are encouraged by it.
- According to St. Anthony, the only guaranteed way to keep demons at bay is with prayer and fasting.

HOW TO SELL YOUR SOUL TO THE DEVIL

1 Wait till the moon is full.
Leave your home when the sun is down and the moon has risen.

2 Travel to a crossroads.
Locate the intersection of two dusty, little-traveled side roads, at the edge of a foreboding wood.

3 Build a fire.
Feed the fire with human or animal bones.

4 Cut yourself.
Cut into your flesh with a small blade, deep enough to release blood but not enough to cause permanent damage.

5 Cast a magic circle.
With a long stick or the toe of one foot, draw a perfect circle in the dirt at the center of the crossroads. Stand within the circle and remain there throughout the Devil's manifestation and presence.

6 Speak an incantation.
Pronounce the words of Aleister Crowley's *Liber Samekh*: "Thou spiritual Sun! Satan! Thou eye, thou lust. Cry aloud! Cry aloud! Whirl the wheel, O my Father, O Satan, O Sun!"

7 Watch for the Devil.
Satan may arrive in a variety of forms, including a dog, goat, talking spool of thread, column of violet flame, or seductive woman dressed all in black.

8 | State your position.
Explain exactly what you are interested in getting from the Devil, be it eternal life, enemy-smiting powers, or unearthly blues-guitar-playing ability.

9 | Entertain the Devil's offer.
He will require you to renounce God and grant him your eternal soul; the rest of the contract, however, is open to significant negotiation.

10 | Cite precedent.
The Devil has granted guided tours of Purgatory and Hell, the power of witchcraft, and riches beyond belief. Demonstrate that you aware of what he has done in the past, and mention that you expect to be treated at least as well.

11 | Write and sign.
Once comfortable with the Devil's offer, write out the terms of the contract backward on parchment. Both you and the Devil must sign with your blood.

Be Aware

- Ancient theological wisdom holds that any act of divination or spell casting requires a pact with the Devil.
- Over the life of the contract, the Devil will act like a pleasant friend and business partner, occasionally granting special powers and so on. However, you should continue to expect that on the date specified in the contract, he will come to harvest your soul with infernal glee.
- In the ancient witch covens, devil pacts were supposedly sealed by eating babies, fornicating with demons in the form of dogs, and kissing the devil's anus.

How to Get Out of a Sold-Soul Contract

⭐ Renounce the contract.
Return to the crossroads, turn your eyes heavenward, and loudly renounce the contract as false and evil.

⭐ Burn the written document.
You may feel physical pain as the unholy pact is consumed by fire.

⭐ Openly declare the Devil to be rejected.
He may laugh at you, but do it anyway: Proclaim loudly in front of respectable witnesses that you repent your congress with the Devil and repudiate it.

⭐ Make restitution.
If your soul-bought power has caused material harm or illness to others, apologize and make whatever restitution you can to your victims.

⭐ Pray.
In rare cases, the Virgin Mary has been known to save the souls of pact makers in the last minutes before death. But don't count on it.

PARANORMAL-BEING IDENTIFICATION

Ghoul	Spirit of an evil dead person, feeds on human beings
Ghost	Spirit of dead person, haunts human beings
Wraith	Vision of a living person, foretells their imminent death
Poltergeist	Invisible ghost, manifest through strange noises
Daemon	Minor god, in the Greek tradition
Demon	Malevolent spirit, either a fallen angel or a spawn of Hell
Devil	Minor evil spirit
The Devil	Supreme evil spirit, God's archenemy
Vampire	Immortal undead, sucks blood of the living
Dhampir	Vampire-human hybrid, all the powers without the weaknesses
Strigoii	Species of vampires found in Romania
Lycanthrope	Evil spirit in the form of a wolf
Werewolf	Human who transforms into a wolf
Fairy	Tiny spirit with magic powers
Faerie	The place where fairies live
Pixie	Mischievous fairy
Gnome	Old-man spirit, guards treasure
Leprechaun	Green-clad dwarf spirit, guards treasure
Brownie	Tiny good-natured spirit, helps with chores
Goblin	Mischievous or evil humanoid creature, cave or forest-dwelling
Hobgoblin	Goblin fond of pranks and causing trouble
Troll	Ugly, slow, dimwitted creature living in a cave; ruins evil discourse on the internet
Bugbear	Bear-shaped goblin that eats wicked children
Manticore	Beast with a man's head, bull-like horns, a lion's body, and a scorpion's tail
Minotaur	Beast with a bull's head and a man's body
Centaur	Beast with the head and trunk of a man and the body of a horse
Satyr	Woodland god, half man and half goat
Sphinx	Beast with the head of a man and body of a lion

HOW TO SURVIVE A ZOMBIE ATTACK

FIRST 24 HOURS

1 Evaluate means of escape.

Access to a vehicle, and the type of vehicle available, will dictate the amount of survival supplies you will be able to bring. If you do not have access to a car or truck, pack lightly so that you will be able to move quickly until you can locate an operating vehicle. Look for humans in operating vehicles or a car in which the human occupants have been killed but the keys are still inside.

2 Gather immediately available survival materials.

- Food: Gather nonperishable foodstuffs as well as perishable food that you will be able to eat before spoilage sets in.
- Communication: Take radios, mobile phones, laptop computers, and batteries.
- Clothing: Pack layers sufficient for sleeping in cold weather, at least one extra pair of shoes or boots, and items that may offer physical protection, such as sports pads or helmets.
- First aid supplies: Empty the contents of your medicine cabinet into a bag and take it with you.
- Weapons: Gun use may be limited by your supply of ammunition, but don't leave these deadly weapons behind. Include long-handled bladed tools or weapons, such as axes or shovels, that may be used to kill zombies while affording you distance of reach. Bludgeoning items, such as baseball bats, will also come in handy.

Power tools are useful only if they have battery charge or fuel; they also tend to be heavy and the weight may not be worth carrying.

- Fuel: Kerosene, gasoline, lighter fluid, lighters, and matches will all be valuable for light and heat; they are also indispensable as additional weapons against zombies, which are flammable and fearful of fire.
- Water: A heavy but vital survival supply; bring as much as you can manage without slowing yourself down, especially if you're traveling on foot.

3 Gather more supplies.

The days immediately following zombie infection will be when supplies are most plentiful—before further infestation complicates access, other human survivors obtain the goods, or they are destroyed (by uncontrolled fires, for example). Obtain more or improved supplies in the above categories from stores or abandoned residences close to your immediate location.

4 Consider including others in your survival plans.

Incorporating other uninfected humans can offer increased security in numbers, but these additional people will also increase the rate at which you consume supplies. Unless their own supplies supplement yours, or their zombie-fighting abilities seem dynamic, ask yourself this question: Are they slowing me down?

5 Trust no one.

Watch for signs of infection when encountering human survivors: Open wounds, bite marks, aggressive confusion, inability to articulate thoughts, and spastic movements are all warning signs of zombification. Flee from or destroy the infected individual by removing its head or

Cover your face to avoid internalizing any zombie gore.

critically damaging the brain with a blade, bullet, or blunt trauma. Uninfected human survivors may in fact be seeking to obtain your survival supplies for themselves.

6 | Avoid splatter.

Do not internalize any matter—blood, flesh, or brains—from a zombie. When destroying zombies, be certain that no gore comes into contact with your eyes, nose, mouth, inner ears, or open wounds. Such contact will result in zombification.

7 | Get out of town.

Opt for less-populated routes out of the city to minimize contact with zombie hordes. Do not stop to comfort any weeping children or helpless wounded, since such isolated figures bear a high chance of being zombies trying to trick you.

8 | Seek out less densely inhabited areas.

Drive as far as possible, as quickly as possible.

First Week

1 Find a safe haven.

Seek out a place to make a secure camp. A city setting is less than ideal; it is easy to be trapped by a horde in an apartment building or in a maze of city streets. A rural area is safer, but may take you too far from contact with other survivors. Drive to a suburb, where you can find a single-family home on about a quarter acre of land. This allows the benefit of an enclosed structure with room to maneuver, as well as a wide vista from which you can spot approaching zombie hordes.

2 Make your haven habitable.

Perform a meticulous sweep, with a gun leveled in front of you, to ensure your new home is free of zombies. Wearing heavy gloves and a mask, remove rotting corpses, being sure to dispose of them far from water sources. If the water taps are working, collect as much water as possible in clean containers, in case the water source later malfunctions. Raid the kitchen, storeroom, and garage for useful supplies. Carefully catalog what you now own.

3 Secure the perimeter.

Nail wood paneling around all windows, lock all doors, and push heavy furniture behind those that swing in. Push a refrigerator or other extremely heavy object over the trap door to the basement, and set a trap of protruding spikes beneath the door from the attic. Outside, use your axe to chop down any trees that could obscure your view of oncoming hordes. Working as quickly as possible to minimize your time outdoors, dig a system of deep trenches across the lawn. Light a fire in the fireplace so that anyone or anything entering via the chimney will fall into the open flame.

4 Set traps.

Zombies are not sophisticated hunters and can be duped into their own destruction with simple traps. Make a recording of talking human voices and bury it in the bushes to draw the zombies into your field of vision; then, open fire on them from a second-story window. Use department store mannequins as decoys to draw the zombies into the trench system you dug in the lawn. Sever the chain of the automatic garage door and rig it to crash down onto zombies entering the garage. Hang a net full of bowling balls over the front door so that a zombie forcing its way in will trigger the balls to rain down and crush its head.

5 Remain vigilant.

Perform daily perimeter checks, peeking out of windows and emerging onto the roof to check for oncoming hordes. Rig walkie-talkies or an old baby safety monitor to alert you to an onslaught. Place a gun under your pillow or clutch it in your hand while sleeping. Do not drink alcohol or become otherwise impaired in any way. Do not relax for even one second.

6 Consume carefully.

Limit food and drink consumption to only the bare caloric minimum so that supplies hold out as long as possible.

7 Remain clued-in.

Build a ham radio to maintain communication with other survivors. Monitor the progress of the infestation, waiting to see if it is improving or worsening and whether the putrefying hordes are approaching your sanctum.

Rig zombie traps around your encampment or building.

8 Add to supplies.

When absolutely necessary, venture forth to find more food, water, and first-aid supplies. When traveling in zombie-infested countryside, keep off main routes of transportation and always travel with several weapons on your person and at the ready. Be prepared to use your weapons against zombies or other noninfected humans who challenge you for your food.

9 Be ready to go.

Keep your essential equipment packed and ready, in a room just off the garage, so that it can be thrown in the trunk at a moment's notice. Leave the car facing out toward the driveway, with the keys in the ignition. The moment it seems you are in danger of being overrun by the horde, floor the accelerator, smash through the garage door, and mow through the pack of zombies, all the while firing your gun through the windshield.

Long Term

1 Put down roots.
Slowly transform your improvised safe haven into a home. Pin up tattered photographs of deceased or zombified friends and loved ones; build permanent structures, such as a gravel driveway, reinforced well, and sanitary outdoor toilet.

2 Teach yourself skills.
Raid abandoned libraries and bookstores to study rainwater filtration, carpentry, car repair, water-borne illness prevention, and other skills you will need to survive long term in a postapocalyptic nightmarescape. Practice martial arts, riflery, horseback riding, and wilderness survival. Learn to hunt and field-butcher animals and to cook over an open flame.

3 Seek out fellow survivors.
Broadcast your location on a ham radio or over wireless networks. Over time the survival equation will tip in favor of groups of humans, rather than individuals, as long as the group is vigilant about protecting the perimeter of its location. Share responsibilities, such as cooking, wound dressing, and zombie killing.

4 Ruthlessly purge infected members of the community.
Make solemn agreements with every member of the group to kill them should they become infected and for them to do the same to you. Doing so will ease everyone's conscience and ensure that there will be no fatal hesitation when the crucial moment comes.

5 Destroy corpses.
If fellow survivors are bitten and must be killed, quickly

destroy their bodies before they can return to life. Wearing a mask and gloves, douse each corpse in kerosene and set it on fire.

6 **Plant crops.**
Most animal life will have disappeared in the zombie plague, but the soil will still yield fruit-bearing trees and vegetables. Defend the perimeter of your fields from zombie invasion until harvest season, and send out harvesters in well-armed teams of two: one to bring in crops, the other to defend against attack. Focus on planting turnips, potatoes, and other root vegetables that can stored for a long time should a crop have to be destroyed or abandoned. Make fruits into preserves so they will last longer.

7 **Record your travails.**
Create a record of anything you learn about the zombies, rates of infection, survival tips, and the names of humans known to have succumbed to the infection. Make multiple digital and hard copies of this record to ensure its availability to future generations or to other surviving groups should your own copy perish during the plague.

8 **Wait out the zombies.**
Zombies cannot survive without feeding on human brains for more than a few weeks, but that countdown does not begin until they have consumed all available humans. Remain in your secure encampment until your wireless communication networks indicate that no zombies have been seen or heard for at least three months.

9 **Reestablish civilization.**
Begin the long process of reconstructing cities, creating a workable government, and developing an economy.

*Rural and semi-rural suburban areas provide several
safety measures against zombies, including open fields of
vision and an abundance of agricultural tools.*

HOW TO OUTRUN A PACK OF ZOMBIES

Depending on the type of plague, the zombies you face will be either "fast" zombies, with roughly human running speed; or "slow" zombies, with impeded speed and motion.

FAST ZOMBIES

1 Get a vehicle.

Escaping the zombies in a car allows you to bring supplies, to vastly outpace your pursuers, and to use the vehicle as a weapon when necessary.

2 Leave morsels.

If you are fleeing fast zombies and encounter other survivors, outpace them and keep the survivors between you and the zombies. Attacking the other survivors will slow the zombies' pace.

3 Trick the zombies.

Travel in circles, double back, and follow no definite pattern as you flee. The zombies are persistent, but not particularly intelligent.

4 Pace yourself.

Expend only as much energy as necessary to get yourself to safety, then rest. You may escape a particular group of zombies, but you must be ready to avoid others. Remember, there will always be more zombies.

Do not attempt to flee zombies by climbing a tree,
as they can wait you out.

Slow Zombies

1 Make a lot of turns.

Zombie hordes, lacking both leaders and functioning brains, tend to move forward as a ragged clump along a straight line. Simply backtracking and making frequent turns can shake loose your followers.

2 Cross water.

Forge a small creek or row across a lake or stream. Slow zombies are terrible swimmers.

3 Set obstacle fires.

Like humans, zombies will avoid fire. Setting a strategic fire line can afford time for escape as the zombies work their way around the line.

4 Climb stairs.

Slow zombies are not good at climbing stairs. If you are absolutely sure there is another means of exit above, climb stairs and, on arriving at a higher story, leap out a window, landing as silently as possible, and sprint away.

All Zombies

1 Stick with the familiar.

Seek escape along routes you know well to avoid becoming disoriented and stumbling into the horde.

2 Do not go up.

Do not climb trees or enter high buildings without any definite path of escape, else you risk becoming entrapped; the zombies will swarm below and simply wait you out. They have nothing better to do.

3 | Do not go underground.
For similar reasons, resist the urge to escape into sewers
or hide in an abandoned well or swimming pool.

4 | Avoid hospitals.
Hospitals are gathering points for sick and dying people,
which means that they will also now be full of zombies.

5 | Do not enter tunnels.
Zombies may enter from the other side, sealing off any
possible escape.

HOW TO KILL A ZOMBIE

1 Burn the zombie.
Burn them with a flamethrower or trick them to wander onto a bonfire. Make sure your zombie-burning heat is more than 400 degrees, so the brain will be putrefied even if the body is not entirely engulfed.

2 Strike the zombie with a blunt object.
Hold a crowbar, two-by-four piece of lumber, or baseball bat tightly with two hands and swing at the zombie's head until its skull cracks and you make direct contact with the brain.

3 Shoot the zombie.
Aim a high-caliber rifle, machine gun, or bazooka directly at the zombie's midsection. When you have slowed or immobilized the zombie with a blast, shoot it a second time in the head.

4 Drive over the zombie with a car.
Gather sufficient speed to knock the zombie down, but don't drive so quickly that you send the zombie flying over the roof of the car.

5 Drive over the zombie with a steamroller.

6 Drive over the zombie with a riding lawnmower.
After you have knocked the zombie down, continue driving over it so that the lawnmower blades chop it into lots of little pieces.

7 | Cut the zombie into bits.
Use a sword, an axe, or the side of a shovel.

8 | Attack the zombie with a chain saw.
First chop off the arms and legs, then slice off the head, and finally carve the skull in half.

9 | Feed the zombie to a wood chipper.
This can be combined with the chain saw by first chopping up the zombie and then pushing it into the wood chipper; alternatively, a whole zombie can be pushed directly into the wood chipper.

Be Aware

- The only part of a zombie you absolutely must destroy is the head. Chopping off other parts may slow the zombie briefly, and may even be fun, but it will not advance your goal.
- The classic zombie-killing method is the chain saw attack, which is extremely effective but also raises the significant issue of zombie splatter. Be careful to avoid allowing any small bits of gore from the chain saw zombie killing to touch your flesh or eyes.
- After killing a zombie, do not reuse the bat, car, lawnmower, wood chipper, ceiling fan, steamroller, chain saw, or shovel until it has been thoroughly cleaned.

How to Immobilize a Zombie

1 Drown the zombie.
Zombies can breathe underwater, but because they will be cut off from food, they will therefore slowly rot. Lay a piece of tarp or sheet over an old well and draw the zombie toward you; jump over the tarp at the last minute and let the zombie run over it. His weight will carry him into the well.

2 Cut off the zombie's legs.
Use your chain saw or axe to hack the legs off the zombie so that it cannot keep shambling toward you.

3 Pin the zombie in place.
Pin the foot of the zombie to the ground with a knitting needle or cleaver, or pin it to a wall with a wooden stake.

4 Entomb the zombies.
Trick the zombies into chasing you into an enclosed space, such as a cave, quarry, or abandoned mine. After escaping, seal off the opening with a triggered detonation, trapping the zombies inside.

5 Capture the zombies in a net.
Toss a fishing net with weighted ends over a single zombie or large group of zombies.

Weapons for Killing Zombies

Weapon	Advantages	Disadvantages
Chain saw	Does a lot of damage very quickly	Can jam with gore; fuel is limited
Dishwasher	Satisfying sound of drowning zombies	Hard to get zombies into dishwasher
Rocks	Endless supply	Not much damage
Sword or axe	Can dismember zombies even when they are not killed	Unwieldy, gets stuck in zombie
Fire or flame	Zombies are highly flammable	May create a larger conflagration
Automobile	Kills several zombies at once	Can damage car
Pistol	Kills zombie with single shot to the head	Requires good aim; ammunition in limited supply
Bow and arrow	Can fashion own arrows	Requires excellent aim
Machine gun	Kills many zombies at once	Rapidly uses up limited stores of ammunition
Hand grenade	Kills many, many zombies at once	Danger to thrower, other nearby survivors
Shovel	Broad side to whack, sharp side to hack	Requires hand-to-hand encounter
Fists	None; last-resort option	Maximizes chances of deadly gore splatter
Baseball bat	Satisfying crunch	Requires powerful upper-arm strength
Steamroller	Extremely effective	Where are you going to get a steamroller?

HOW TO COMMUNICATE WITH A ZOMBIE SPOUSE

⭐ Set boundaries.
Shackle or chain your undead spouse to an anchored and immovable object to prevent lashing out or unpleasant surprises.

⭐ Be patient.
Generally, zombification results in not only brain degeneration but also the deterioration of the tongue and other muscles and organs associated with speech. Even if intelligible, your spouse may take much longer to communicate thoughts and feelings. Don't interrupt or cut off your spouse midstatement.

⭐ Listen for subtext.
When she says "Braaaaaains . . . braaaaaains . . . ." she may mean, "I love you, but I'm trapped inside this zombie body."

⭐ Accept diminishing intimacy.
Physical contact for zombies is related almost entirely to brain eating, and sexual relations can be relatively limited after flesh rotting commences. Remind yourself that it's not about you, it's about the inevitable putrefaction neither of you has chosen.

⭐ Don't be jealous.
Once zombified, your partner will likely want to spend most of her time with "the horde" rather than at home with you.

Set clear boundaries for this new phase of your relationship.

⭐ Use "I feel" statements.

Don't pressure your zombie spouse by implicating her in your anger. Say things like, "I feel hurt when you try to crack open my skull and eat my brains."

⭐ Allow ample space.

When your spouse tries to eat you, give her plenty of space.

⭐ Be assertive.

Don't be afraid to stand up for yourself and clearly state your feelings, if necessary by wielding a chain saw or bat.

Be Aware

In most municipalities, discovering that one's spouse is undead is grounds for annulment.

WHAT TO EXPECT IF YOU'VE BEEN BITTEN

Right away: Area around bite begins to swell and throb. Apply a tourniquet to limit blood loss.

Within ten minutes: Hair begins to fall out in clumps, pustules break out around bite. Rapidly drink three liters of fresh water to counter bite toxicity by flushing out your system.

Within half an hour: Contagion is spreading rapidly: Hair has fallen out except a few patches; pustules cover entire body; numbness in extremities.

Within one hour: Nausea, disorientation, newfound appetite for human flesh.

Within five hours: Nausea and disorientation gone, entire body numb, insensible to pain or discomfort. Total disinterest in previous friends, hobbies; all interest and attention focused on desire for human flesh, especially brains.

Within ten hours: Entire body is putrefying; desire to eat brains intense and undeniable. Seek out other zombies to form a horde and hunt for the living.

CHAPTER 2

CREATURE FEATURES

HOW TO HUNT AND KILL A WEREWOLF

1 Assemble a group.

Many, but not all, werewolves hunt in packs; you'll want to do the same. Choose people to join you on the hunt who have experience in the outdoors, with hunting, and with firearms. Be clear and honest with them about the nature of your hunt; if they are expecting to be hunting natural rather than supernatural prey, they are likely to become terrified and useless to you when the beast actually appears.

2 Be sure it is a werewolf.

Unless you have actually seen someone undergo the transformation, there is simply no way to be sure that any given human is the werewolf you're looking for. While it is true that they have a tendency to go shirtless to stay cool, so do normal human bodybuilders, surfers, and fashion models. Werewolves, meanwhile, live discreet daily lives as everything from students and doctors to talk show hosts and R&B singers; they make their homes everywhere from the forests of America's Pacific Northwest to the streets of London's SoHo district. And even if you get lucky and correctly identify one, you probably don't know who their revenge-minded packmates are.

3 Await the full moon.

Lycanthropy—the power to shape-shift—is at its weakest in the new moon phase of the lunar cycle. However it is also most likely at this time that werewolves will remain in human form, creating uncertainty about the identity of your target. While werewolves are strongest in their power at the full moon, they are also least in control of it, and will have more limited ability to assume human form or entertain human trains of thought once they have transformed. This can be used to your advantage, in that you can anticipate that the creature will act more purely from animal instinct than from human strategy.

4 | Retrain yourself to nocturnal rhythms.

Adjust your sleep schedule beginning a week before the full moon so that you are awake as little as possible during the day and as long as possible during the night, taking time off work if necessary. Exercise and remain mentally and physically active during these times.

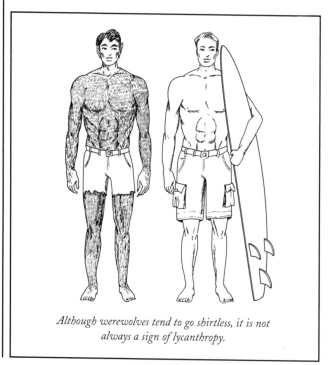

Although werewolves tend to go shirtless, it is not always a sign of lycanthropy.

5 Establish a stakeout.

Situate yourselves in the area around where your target lives, if you think you know its human identity, or where it hunts, if you are unsure who the creature might be. Work in pairs and seek vantage points that are protected from at least one side—in the city, using buildings or vehicles; in the woods, using natural features such as rock, or using a hunter's blind. Remain in contact with the other groups using phones or walkie-talkies, but only make contact on sighting of the werewolf. Otherwise remain quiet.

6 Set bait.

In wooded areas, tether a bait animal such as a deer in a clearing that is under the watch of your group. The werewolf will be able to smell and sense the presence of your group, but it may still find the prospect of the deer difficult to resist, especially if it has been some time since it has last fed.

7 Use silver weapons.

Consumption of silver can be poisonous to any regular human; long-term exposure can seriously impact nervous system function, causing softening of brain tissue, mental agitation to the point of uncontrollable rage, and shooting pain throughout the body. Because the werewolf's nervous system already exists in a state of extreme flux, driving two wildly different physiologies at once, the effects of silver poisoning are multiplied exponentially. Introducing silver to the werewolf's body via bullet, blade, or pill will quickly result in extensive damage or death. It is important to use silver, rather than other toxic substances, because silver's close association with the moon gives it a special affinity in the lycanthrope's system; the werewolf's bodily defenses seem almost to welcome it as familiar, thus insinuating the poison deeply and more effectively.

8 Use wolfsbane.

Aconitum vulparia or wolfsbane, an herb with dark green leaves and colorful hood-shaped flower petals, is another effective deterrent proven fatally poisonous both to humans and wild wolves—and thus doubly so to werewolves. Direct contact with its leaves, or in the form of smoke (leaves thrown on a fire) or steam (brewed in boiling water) can injure or repel the creature; inhalation of its fumes will wreak havoc on a werewolf's circulation, often triggering his transformation while simultaneously disrupting his voluntary motor control. Consumption of a wolfsbane potion will usually be fatal.

9 Dispose of the body.

Because a werewolf upon death will revert to human form, anyone who might come into contact with the body will misunderstand the circumstances as one of murder rather than of supernatural combat. Take steps to conceal and then bury the body of the former werewolf for your own protection and out of respect for the human life that had been eclipsed by the lycanthropic curse.

Be Aware

- Anyone bitten by a werewolf and survives will eventually turn into a werewolf. There is no known cure.
- An otherwise normal human being covered in hair may suffer not from lycanthropy, but congenital hypertrichosis, a condition that causes excess hair growth.

HOW TO ADJUST TO BEING A WEREWOLF

1 Consider your livelihood.

Your life will be disrupted like clockwork for a three-day period centering on the full moon every twenty eight days. Choose a living situation, therefore, that will accommodate your needs. Self-employment is preferable to the constant need to explain to a boss that your vacation days are not flexible; explore careers as a massage therapist, business consultant, artist, craftsman, or freelance writer.

2 Consider your relationship status.

Marriage to a non-lycanthrope is problematic for the same reason as holding a job. Remain single or mate with another werewolf, if possible. If you are determined to marry a human, pick one who is not an investigative reporter.

3 Join a pack.

Seek out other werewolves with whom to form a pack. Although werewolves who meet each other in human form can send subtle but unmistakable signals to one another, your "wolf-dar" may not be very well tuned if you have recently transformed. The surest way to find lycanthropic friends is to do so in wolf form: the night before the full moon, go camping in an unpopulated forest (old-growth forests are best). When you transform to your bestial shape and run wild in the excitement of the predatory hunt, stay alert for other wolves; when you meet them; make friendly overtures and join forces to hunt together. Do not mate until you've made sure your new friend is an actual werewolf, not just a big smart timber wolf. Puppies could be embarrassing.

4 | Hide in plain sight.

Sometimes the riskiest strategies are the most effective. Join a team of professional vampire hunters. Your keen, wolflike senses will aid you greatly in the art of pursuing and staking the undead; you stand an excellent chance of becoming your team's most valuable member. Because vampire hunting is an underground activity, you can simply be unavailable for expeditions that coincide with your full-moon cycle. If your teammates do discover your secret, point to your kind's ancient animosity toward vampires and explain that this instinct puts you firmly on *their* side of the supernatural wars. You are a living, hot-blooded mammal who just wants to get along.

WHAT TO EXPECT IF YOU'VE BEEN BITTEN

Right away: Throbbing pain and flowing blood at the bite location.

Within two hours: Wooziness, loss of strength, disorientation as with flu or immunological illness.

One to three days: Continued throbbing at wound site; beginnings of new hair growth on body and face.

Two to three days: Substantial new hair growth all over body and face. Teeth take on new, canine look and feel. Keen desire for red meat.

Next full moon: Transformation into full wolf; insatiable desire to feed on animals or humans, as available.

HOW TO BUILD A MONSTER FROM SPARE PARTS

1 Locate a mountain castle.

Find a castle where you can work undisturbed, away from nosy villagers but with close access to graveyards.

2 Hire an assistant.

Digging up graves is hard physical labor. An assistant with a strong back, even if hunched, will be invaluable in excavating the necessary body parts.

3 Gather your materials.

What's true in many craft and construction activities is also true here: The quality of your materials drives the quality of your results. Find the freshest by seeking out newly dug graves, which are indicated by large quantities of flowers or groups of weeping mourners. Dig at night by the light of the moon. Take the whole corpse (you never know how you might need to kit it out for parts later on) and restore the gravesite to resemble the state in which you found it to avoid suspicion.

4 Keep parts preserved until you're ready to stitch them together.

Avoid the danger of postexhumation rot by storing body parts on a snow bank or in a freezing underground dungeon until you have secured all the necessary pieces and have enough time to build the body properly.

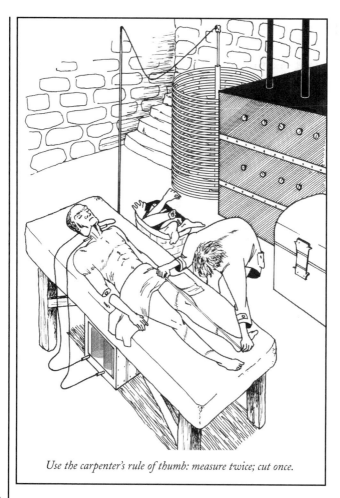

Use the carpenter's rule of thumb: measure twice; cut once.

5 Measure twice; cut once.

Measure your incisions and dismemberments twice before using your saw. The effort spent in ensuring that each cut is made exactly as you want it will save time by avoiding having to acquire replacement parts.

6 Stitch and rivet carefully.

The human body is an unimaginably intricate and delicate network of interlocking systems. Unless you are a trained surgeon, in which case your success rate at this task is at least 50 percent higher, you will be aligning these systems on a rough macroscopic level and then trusting the sheer power of violent electricity to fuse the messy bits together. Make your sutures tight and close together with a well-rated surgical thread, and solder the neck-bolted electrodes firmly into place, extending an inch into muscle tissue beneath the cauterized skin.

7 Watch the weather reports.

Wait for a raging thunderstorm. Pay attention to forecasts a few hours in advance—better to be doing your prep work before the rain starts.

8 Activate the body.

Strap your undead creation to a table with leather shackles. Position the table to face an open window. Using extralong jumper cables, attach the monster's electrode bolts to the lightning rod affixed to the roof, wrapping them securely to the rod with heavy electrical tape. Wait for a lightning bolt to strike the rod, sending electricity surging through the wires and galvanizing the creature's nervous system into first reflexive and then sustainable activity. That is: life. *Life!*

9 Laugh maniacally.

Lean back, clutch at the sky, and cackle.

10 Relax and enjoy your success.

Nothing can possibly go wrong now.

How to Build a Bride For Your Monster

1 Look for signs of loneliness in your original creation.
Signs of romantic yearning in a man-monster include moaning, wandering listlessly through the grounds of the castle, and the murder of hapless innocents.

2 Assess your monster's parameters for a desirable mate.
Beyond the spark of electricity, you will also want to ensure that the spark of chemistry bring your monster's new relationship to life. Since the Myers-Briggs personality assessment is less effective as a mating metric for the reanimated than for the still living, measure your creature's more relevant character traits using the similar, four-part Frankenstein-Igor assessment: I/E (impressively large vs. elegantly petite), N/S (nonspeaking vs. speaking), F/T (freshly dead vs. time lapsed), P/J (parts assembled vs. just one corpse).

3 Find suitable parts.
Take a brain that's roughly the same size as your monster's brain to avoid his feeling "not smart enough" for his new companion.

4 Animate the bride.
Follow the same steps as for the original monster.

5 Choose an appropriate honeymoon destination.
Anyplace requiring air travel is not feasible. Secluded lakeside cabins are hard to beat: lovely scenery, expectations of privacy, no elaborate tourist activities. Just be sure there are no gregarious neighbor children.

HOW TO SURVIVE
WITH SCISSOR HANDS

1 Keep to yourself.
Cultivate an aura of eccentric shyness. Do not try to explain your situation in your halting, broken half-speech, or to cast blame on the mad scientist who created you.

2 Inspire wonderment.
Temper the villagers' natural discomfort with your scissor hands by using them to create whimsical topiary sculptures and a hedge labyrinth.

3 Identify a potential romantic partner.
Find someone whose shy, artistic temperament, limited social skills, and sense of otherness are a metaphorical counterpart to your scissor-handedness.

4 Earn the trust and love of the romantic partner.
Explore the physical aspects of your love, but stop after first base.

5 Parlay that trust into the trust of the community.
Win over the locals by cutting their hair. Use your finger blades as shish-kebabs at the next community barbecue.

6 Restrain your temper.
Resist the urge to impale those who mock you.

7 Celebrate being different.
Show the townspeople, by virtue of your kindness and simple humanity, that being unusual is not equivalent to being evil.

8 Find a new mad scientist.
Ask the new scientist to correct your bizarre handicap. Pay any price.

*Use your scissor hands to enhance your
neighborhood social status.*

9 Become adept with your new, "normal" hands.
Ask your new friends to demonstrate such activities as picking things up, scratching yourself, and eating with utensils.

10 Mourn what's been lost.
Contemplate how maybe, just maybe, it was better to be different but special than to be the same as all the others.

HOW TO BUILD A FAIRY TRAP

1 Cut or drill a small hole in the corner of a cardboard shoebox.

2 Decorate the box.
Adorn the inside and outside of the shoebox and lid with colorful glitter and paint. Choose your color scheme, depending on the type of fairy you wish to trap: pink and red for flower fairies, yellow and orange for garden fairies, blue and purple for evening fairies, and green and brown for woodland fairies.

3 Make furniture for the box.
Construct a little bed from an empty matchbox, make pillows out of dandelion heads, and add a bit of tissue for a blanket. Spools of thread of varying sizes can be used for a table and chairs. Clip photographs of flowers, animals, and pretty things from magazines and tape them to the shoebox walls.

4 Leave the box for the fairy to discover.
Place the box trap outdoors 20 feet from one side of your house, near a corner, so that you can view it by peeking around the corner.

5 Set the trap.
Tie one end of a 25-foot length of string to the middle of a sharpened pencil. Set the pencil point-side up in the middle of the shoebox; prop the lid of the box on the tip of the pencil and run the extra string through a hole and out the box so that it ends around the corner of the house, out of sight of the box.

6 | Gain the fairy's trust.
Sit beside the box for 10 minutes each day and say aloud in a yearning, childlike voice how much you wish you had a fairy for a friend, how much you would love the fairy, and how much fun you and the fairy would have together.

7 | Bait the trap.
Leave a small sweet treat such as a marshmallow, gumdrop, or golden thimbleful of honey in the box each night after you have expressed your wish for the fairy to come.

8 | Be patient.
The reaction time for an alert or startled fairy is similar to that of a hummingbird, but a relaxed fairy moves at a much slower speed. Do not try to spring the trap the first time the fairy visits the box. Allow the fairy to become comfortable with the trap, spending time in the box and eating the sweets for several nights, lulling her into letting down her guard. You will be able to tell when the fairy is inside by the luminous sparkles dancing in the air around the box.

9 | Hide.
After the fairy has become comfortable enough to sleep inside her little bed, take the loose end of the string and go hide around the corner from the fairy trap. Peer around the corner. When the fairy settles in for the night, pull the string, dislodging the pencil and dropping the box top, thus entrapping the fairy.

10 | Make sure the fairy is not a demon in disguise.
Demons cannot bear to have the word "goodness" pass their lips. Demand that the fairy say the word. If she cannot, release the tiny demon and apologize for the mistake.

11 Present work to your fairy in the form of play.

Your fairy excels naturally at certain tasks. Invite her enthusiastic cooperation—using more sugary treats—in taking on "games" for you, such as delivering messages, spying discreetly on others, and decorating for parties.

Be Aware

- It is most effective to make your own fairy-trap furniture from scratch rather than using dollhouse furniture. Fairies appreciate hand-craftiness.

- If the magical creature in your trap has no wings and is dressed in an all-brown peasant ensemble, with a cocked hat, you have caught a brownie: a cousin to the fairy that is of similar good humor but physically resembles a small goblin. You may choose to release it or force it to do chores.

- If at any time you no longer wish to keep the fairy, you may make her disappear by no longer believing in her.

HOW TO CATCH A UNICORN

1 Journey into the heart of the forest.
Venture forth with companions brave and true, on a perfect sky-blue day, to a verdant forest of towering oaks, where the swaying flowers of the green meadow are kissed by the midday sun.

2 Find the path of the unicorn.
Seek the trail of unnaturally beautiful flowers that have sprung up where the hooves of the unicorn have trod.

3 Seek the purest of streams.
When the path of flowers leads to a burbling stream, taste of it. Water that is perfectly, supernaturally clean and fresh shows where a unicorn has recently quenched its thirst and purified the stream with the magic of its horn.

4 Listen for happy animal noises.
Forest animals of all kinds are made joyful and pleasant by the nearness of a unicorn.

5 Deploy your virgin.
Invite a young virginal maiden, with flowers woven into her hair and a basket of fruit by her side, to sit in a clearing, cross-legged, singing gaily to herself. Together with your companions brave and true, hide behind a rock.

6 Wait for the unicorn to fall asleep.
The unicorn will soon respond to the virgin's pure song and emerge from the forest to walk slowly toward her. Eventually, the unicorn will place its head in the maiden's lap and fall asleep.

7 Guide the unicorn home.
Gently ease a golden cord around the animal's neck and have the maiden lead it to a secluded garden.

8 Feed and care for the unicorn.
Generally speaking, unicorns will feed as do other ruminants, and will be happy on a diet of grasses, weeds, and hay. In its secret bower, the unicorn should have access to outdoors areas as well as to indoor shelter, and be able to move freely within these boundaries. Tethered unicorns become listless and sullen.

9 Guard the unicorn.
Keep it safe and secret from those who may become jealous of your magical pet, or who are drawn to it by following the rainbows that will beam from the unicorn when it is especially happy. So long as the unicorn is happy, it will stay with you. It will be your duty to protect it from any who would do it harm.

Be Aware

- The Unicorn Tapestries, a collection of seven tapestries that dates from the Middle Ages, are preserved at the Metropolitan Museum of Art in the historic Cloisters. These artifacts can be consulted for details about appropriate dress and weaponry for classical unicorn hunting. Venturing forth with a party of at least a dozen armed men, using greyhounds to chase by sight, and running hounds to chase by scent.
- Unicorn liver is believed to cure leprosy and prevent disease, but obtaining it will cause the death of the unicorn.
- Only a virgin maiden will be able to ride a unicorn.

Use a virginal maiden for bait and wait for the unicorn to relax.

HOW TO RESIST A SIREN SONG

1 Keep a good lookout.

Sirens resemble beautiful young women with the wings and lower bodies of birds; they are found on flowery islands with rocky shores. Keep watch by using a powerful terrestrial telescope (or spyglass) to ensure that you see the sirens before you hear their supernaturally beautiful, yet highly dangerous, singing.

2 Fill your ears with wax.

Into each ear, jam a teaspoon of recently melted candle wax (heat till soft and let cool for 30 seconds) or newly harvested beeswax.

3 Set your boat on autopilot.

Trim the mainsail close to centerline, reducing wind area; next, engage an automated gyrocompass to propel the ship forward in a straight line through the rocky strait or until safely past the sirens' island.

4 Tie yourself to the mast.

Connect one end of a short piece of towline to your ankle with a tightly pulled slipknot; tie the other end to the base of the mast.

5 Play competing music.

As the sirens' music intensifies, pump the onboard stereo to full volume. Alternatively, order the most talented musician on board to play his lute or lyre as loudly as possible to drown out the enchanting singing of the sirens.

Secure yourself to the boat and play music to drown out sirens.

6 Celebrate victory.

On failing to bewitch a passerby, a siren is traditionally obligated to commit suicide by flinging herself into the water.

Be Aware

- Sailors who are tempted by the sirens' song unwittingly pilot their ships toward the sirens and wreck their boats against the cliffs. The sirens then fish the bodies from the water and feast upon the flesh of the dead.
- Sirens are almost always found in groups of three or more.

VARIOUS CRYPTOZOOLOGICAL CREATURES

Creature:

Alias	Territory	Appearance
Yeti: The Abominable Snowman	The snowy peaks of the Himalayas	Giant white ape that walks like a man
Bigfoot: Sasquatch	The forests of the Pacific Northwest	Giant brown ape that walks like a man
Loch Ness Monster: Nessie	The murky waters of Loch Ness, Scotland	Giant plesiosaur-like serpent
Mokele-Mbembe: "Stopper of rivers"	The fertile lands of the Congo River basin, Africa	Elephantine water creature with elongated neck
The Jersey Devil: The 13th Leeds child	The harsh scrub-foliage of New Jersey's Pine Barrens	Head of a horse, body of a male human, bat wings
El Chupacabra: "The goat sucker"	The dark nights of Puerto Rico and the American Southwest	Spiny-backed reptile
Kraken: Cthulhu's little brother	The depths of the Atlantic Ocean	Like a squid, but…
Howler Monkey Snake: Guariba-boia	Beneath the soil of northeastern Brazil	Head of monkey, body of boa constrictor
Mongolian Death Worm: Allghoi khorkoi	The sands of the southern Gobi desert	A living, crawling, fat, blood-red intestine
Mothman: None	The town of Point Pleasant, West Virginia	Gray humanoid with mothlike wings, glowing eyes
Thunderbird: Roc	Worldwide	Lizardlike winged creature

Size	Notable for
Seven feet tall	Identified by long, yaklike hair and parasites in its feces
Six to seven feet tall	Last extant member of species *Gigantopithecus*
Indeterminate size somewhere between alligator and sailing ship	Has been photographed with sonar technology
Size of a large hippopotamus	Flesh fatal to those who consume it
Man-sized	Mascot of a hockey team
Small-bear-sized	Hops like a bunny, eats livestock
…Ten times larger	Engages in undersea combat with sperm whales
Twenty feet long	Emits terrifying roar from below the Earth's surface
Two to five feet long	Sprays fatal acid, shoots electric charge
Four feet tall	Haunts the abandoned TNT factory outside town
Bigger than an elephant	Creates thunder with wing-flaps

121. *various cryptozoological creatures*

HOW TO RECOGNIZE WHEN AN INVISIBLE PERSON HAS ENTERED THE ROOM

1 Watch for a floating pair of eyes.
The adjusted-refractive-index method most often used to render people invisible leaves the retinas visible to prevent the invisible person from becoming blind.

2 Turn on the lights.
Other methods of invisibility leave the subject opaque with respect to the sun and other light sources. Turn on all the lights and look for uncast shadows moving across the floor.

3 Watch the floorboards.
Invisible people are not weightless, and their movements will create small indentations on the floor or footprints in deep carpet. If you are outdoors, watch for new footprints in the soil, sand, or grass.

4 Look for moving objects.
Watch for things being lifted out of pockets, doors opening and closing by themselves, bubble wrap popping of its own accord, and so on.

5 Listen for new sounds.
Be attentive to apparently unsourced coughs, sneezes, and sighs, or the scrape of chair legs.

Spray dry powder through the room to coat an invisible person with visible particles.

6 Sniff the air.
Note new smells that have entered the room, such as perfumes, colognes, soaps, and body odor.

7 Observe animal behavior.
If a dog suddenly bristles, growls, and points, follow his lead to the invisible person.

8 Spray a visible fluid.
Fill a large spray bottle or water pistol with milk, cream, or other opaque fluid. Saturate the air suddenly and look for the human-shaped mass of mess stumbling around. Also useful in this manner: a fire extinguisher, a bag of flour, a clown's confetti cannon.

9 Swing a broom.
Take a broom, mop, crutch, flagpole, or other handy long-handled item and sweep the air vigorously. Listen for startled cries of pain.

Be Aware

- Many invisible people have felonious or voyeuristic intent. Be on the lookout especially for invisible people in banks, jewelry stores, and bedrooms.
- Doors opening and shutting on their own may indicate a demon or ghost instead of an invisible person.

HOW TO SURVIVE IF THERE ARE CHILDREN IN YOUR CORN

1 Cull.
Widen your rows so that the children are more visible as they wander among the corn.

2 Spray.
Liberally hose the cornfield with holy water, which has a proven effectiveness against demon children.

3 Introduce natural predators.
Employ what agriculturalists call "biological controls," i.e., a stronger, more powerful animal to control the infestation. Purchase a lion or other big cat to prowl through your cornfield and eat the corn children.

4 Fence the perimeter.
Enclose the perimeter of the field with barbed-wire fencing, topped with crosses to repulse further infestation.

5 Reconvert the children.
Employing a priest or team of deacons and a wading pool full of holy water, rebaptize the captured corn children and convert them from the pagan death cult they have joined.

6 Raze the fields.
Permanently rid your fields of children by burning the existing stalks and letting the field lie fallow for a season. When replanting, rotate the crop of corn with soybeans instead; resume planting corn the following season.

7 Flee.

If children reappear when you next grow corn, immediately abandon your field, your home, and your town, leaving behind half-drunk cups of coffee, open magazines, and tumbleweeds slowly spinning through the dusty streets.

Be Aware

- Signs of children in your corn include a devastated crop, bent stalks, and the corpses of townsfolk trussed up and displayed as scarecrows with their eyes sewn shut.
- Corn children most likely have been converted via demonic possession to the worship of a pagan antichrist named He Who Walks Between the Rows.
- While your corn is infested with children, alert passersby with large, highly visible signage stating that they must not stop or slow down while passing your fields, even if they run over a body.

CHAPTER 3

COSMIC CRISES

HOW TO SURVIVE AN ALIEN ABDUCTION

1 Remain calm.

Aliens who abduct human beings rarely exert permanent physical harm on their victims. The best strategy is to remain calm and endure the experience without resistance.

2 Cover your eyes.

Press the inside of your elbow tightly over your face to shield your eyes from the painfully bright white lights that accompany abduction.

3 Focus on remaining conscious.

Nearly all abductees are rendered insensible during the period of abduction and only recover the memory later. Maintain active awareness by pinching yourself or digging your nails into your thighs. Chant, "I am awake, I am alive, I am awake, I am alive," as you are tractor-beamed or ushered up the staircase of light that leads onto the ship.

4 Be observant.

Noting every aspect of the ship's interior, including the color and shape of the aliens themselves, will distract your mind from its terror and increase your ability to later communicate the details of your experience.

5 Be cooperative.

Obey the aliens' instructions, which may range from removing your false teeth to learning an alien language or even making love to an alien.

Remember to shield your eyes from the blinding lights of alien technology.

6 | Call someone.
When the aliens deposit you back on Earth, immediately contact a friend or law-enforcement official to report your experience. The longer you wait, the less likely you are to be believed.

7 | Spread the message.
Tell as many people as possible any warnings the aliens have asked you to communicate.

HOW TO THWART AN ALIEN ABDUCTION

1 Hide your fear.

The extraterrestrial biological entity (EBE) may sense your fear and act rashly.

2 Control your thoughts.

Think of nothing violent or upsetting—the EBE may have the ability to read your mind. Try to avoid mental

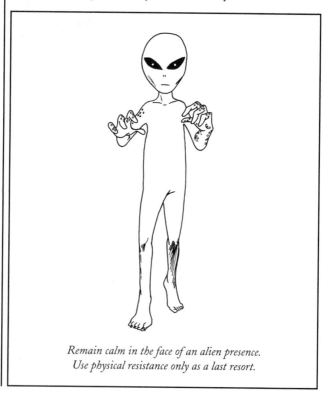

Remain calm in the face of an alien presence.
Use physical resistance only as a last resort.

images of abduction (boarding the saucer, anal probes); such images may encourage them to take you.

3 | Resist verbally.
Firmly tell the EBE to leave you alone.

4 | Resist mentally.
Picture yourself enveloped in a protective shield of white light or in a safe place. Telepathic EBEs may get the message.

5 | Resist physically.
Physical resistance should be used only as a last resort. Attack the EBE's eyes (if they have any)—you will not know what its other, more sensitive areas are.

Be Aware

- Abduction experiences generally follow a seven-step model: capture, examination, conference, tour, journey, return, and aftermath.
- Approximately half of Americans believe in the existence of UFOs, and one in ten claims to have seen one.
- People most likely to be abducted include those with a history of terrestrial abduction in their family, those living in wealthy Western countries, and those who have already been abducted by aliens.
- Abductions occur most frequently in the summer months and in those weeks following the airing of a popular alien-related television show or film.
- Some ufologists argue that UFOs come not from outer space but from another dimension, from the future, or from the center of the Earth.

CLOSE ENCOUNTERS BY KIND

Encounter Number	Description	How You Know You've Had One
Close Encounter of the First Kind (CE1)	Sighting of UFO	You see strange lights or a flying saucer
Close Encounter of the Second Kind (CE2)	UFO has effect on environment	In presence of UFO, your car stalls or becomes superheated; you are paralyzed
Close Encounter of the Third Kind (CE3)	Aliens emerge from UFO	You see an alien being
Close Encounter of the Fourth Kind (CE4)	Abduction	You are brought aboard an alien ship or you experience a gap in memory and wake with physical scars and painful and confusing memories
Close Encounter of the Fifth Kind (CE5)	Human-initiated contact	Using communication devices or telepathy, you send/receive messages with aliens
Close Encounter of the Sixth Kind (CE6)	Alien attack	After a CE2 or CE3, you have a major, life-threatening injury or are dead
Close Encounter of the Seventh Kind (CE7)	Human-alien hybridization	Following a CE4, you discover yourself to be pregnant with an alien baby

HOW TO RECOVER REPRESSED ABDUCTION MEMORY

1 Note gap in memory.
The hallmark of a repressed alien-abduction memory is a chunk of time, usually two or more hours, missing from the normal recollection of experience, for which no other explanation, such as alcohol-related blackout, can be identified.

2 Confirm abduction by presence of emotional and physical phenomena.
Abductees can have inexplicable scars or bruises, a strong positive or negative emotional reaction to photographs of UFOs, and a newfound fear of dwarfs, clowns, or other dysmorphic humans or humanoids.

3 Create a safe environment.
Begin the process of hypnosis by replacing electric lights with candlelight, putting on calming music or electronically generated wave sounds, and sitting upright in a comfortable position on a chair or sofa.

4 Activate a recording device.
Use a digital audio recorder with a plug and a battery backup.

5 Enter a state of "total body relaxation."

Breathe deeply and slowly in and out, exhaling stressors and anxiety and breathing in peace, until you find your mind clear of thoughts and slip into a peaceful state of semiconsciousness.

6 Journey back to the abduction.

Guided by "repressed-memory prompts" from a friend, explore the abduction incident. The friend should slowly list the common abduction-experience imagery, such as bright white lights, shimmering fields of stars, and medical exam rooms.

7 Allow the memories to surface.

When one of the prompts strikes a familiar chord, begin to speak, as if telling a story with yourself as the protagonist. As you talk, more and more details will return to you until the full memory takes shape in your mind.

8 Return to a safe place.

If the memories become too intense, stop speaking and breathe deeply 10 times, until you feel calm enough to continue.

9 Conclude the session.

When you have fully relived your abduction experience, remain in your peaceful semiconscious state for 10 minutes or more, breathing deeply and imagining yourself in a "happy place," such as a beach or childhood home, until you feel safe and calm enough to open your eyes and return to real life.

10 | Evaluate.

Play back what's been recorded. Review the memories that were brought up and judge whether they sound familiar and true. Listen for the intrusion of alien voices, or yourself speaking in an alien language, in the middle of the story. Compare notes with other abductees to see if what happened to you resonates with their experiences.

Be Aware

- Approximately one in four abductees report that the aliens cautioned them, at the time of abduction or subsequently, not to try to remember what happened.
- Many abductees describe the memory-recovery process as emotionally wrenching but ultimately satisfying, allowing them to return to normal life.
- Some mental health experts suggest that hypnosis in fact creates false memories by strongly suggesting the imagery it claims to recover. Some ufologists, however, suggest that these mental health experts are themselves part of the alien conspiracy.
- Between 10 and 25 percent of abductees recover their memories spontaneously, without recourse to hypnosis.

KINDS OF ALIENS

Name	Appearance	Typical Attitude
Grays	Four feet tall, gray or green, small bodies with big heads and large single-colored eyes, three or four fingers	Inquisitive
Neonates	Three to four feet tall, fetuslike faces, disproportionately large heads, similar to grays but with visibly differentiated pupils	Inquisitive, highly intelligent
Felinoids	Five to six feet tall, vaguely humanoid cats with long fingernails	Warlike, predatory
Nordics	Six feet tall, silent blonde humanoids	Distant, unspeaking
Blobs	Ever-growing, thick gelatinous mass	Acquisitive
Orions	Human-sized, dark-haired, almond-shaped eyes	Warlike
Alpha Centaurians	Human-sized, with gills and webbed feet and hands, blue-gray	Consciousness-raising
Arcturians	Seven to eight feet tall, dark brown, horselike but with long, thin fingers	Peace-loving
Mantises	Six feet tall, large bug eyes, insect frames, slender bodies	Kind and gentle unless provoked, in which case their vicious response is not personal
Reptilians (or reptoids)	Seven feet tall, bright red eyes, lizardlike	Cruel, domineering
Alf	Three feet tall, big-nosed, fuzzy	Wry, wisecracking

HOW TO MAKE AN EFFECTIVE TINFOIL HAT

1 Measure your head.
Gather the dimensions of your scalp using a soft tape measure, measuring from the middle of your forehead to the base of your skull.

2 Unroll tinfoil.
Using clean, premium-brand foil that has not been used to wrap food, measure double the length from your forehead to skull, plus four inches. Detach the foil using the serrated edge of the box and fold the foil in half, shiny side facing out.

3 Mold the hat to your head.
Carefully place the sheet of foil over your head and scrunch it down to follow the shape of your skull, as would a shower cap or helmet. If any exposed scalp remains, attach additional pieces of foil to cover; adhere using clear tape.

4 At each temple, poke a quarter-inch hole on either side of the foil.

5 Create a chin strap.
Unroll an additional three-inch strip of foil and fold it over twice, creating a durable, double-folded chin strap.

Measure enough fresh tinfoil to wrap around your head.

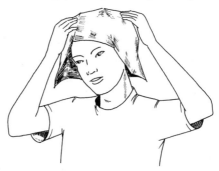

Mold the foil to the unique contours of your skull.

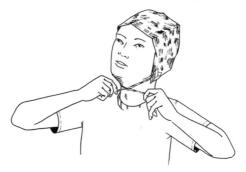

*Form a chin strap from a double-sided strip of foil;
attach with tape and tie.*

6 Thread the chin strap through the holes and attach with clear tape.

7 Don your hat.
Wear your hat in any place and anytime you wish to screen your thoughts from extraterrestrial-alien, governmental, or other types of surveillance.

Be Aware
- Tinfoil hats are based on science: A layer of aluminum protects whatever lies beneath it from radio-frequency electromagnetic radiation.
- For maximum protection, wrap foil around not just the head, but the entire face and skull.

HOW TO PROJECT YOURSELF ON THE ASTRAL PLANE

1 Prepare your environment.
Find somewhere you can be totally alone. Turn off your phone and any other electronic devices and distractions. Dim the lights.

2 Prepare your body.
Remove jewelry, loosen clothing, and lie down comfortably on the floor, with your body along a north-south axis. Cover yourself with a blanket.

3 Pre-remember.
Tell yourself five times, in a soothing voice, "I will remember all that is about to happen."

4 Relax.
Take deep calming breaths. Think of pleasing scenery. Let anxieties slip away.

5 Enter the hypnagogic state.
Raise one forearm slightly while leaving the upper part of your arm on the ground. Drift toward sleep, until the falling of your forearm jerks you back to wakefulness. Repeat until you slip into a state of semiconsciousness.

6 Stare at the darkness.
Think of nothing. Be alone with the nothingness.

7 Feel the vibration.
Concentrate on the void that lies before you until you feel a mild vibration travel through your body.

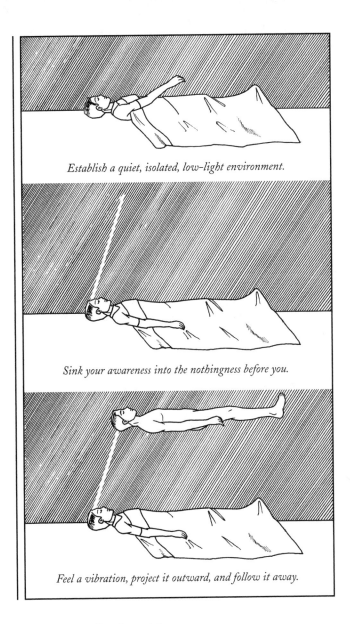

Establish a quiet, isolated, low-light environment.

Sink your awareness into the nothingness before you.

Feel a vibration, project it outward, and follow it away.

8 Control the vibration.

Mentally seize the tingling and force it into different parts of your body.

9 Project the vibration.

Pick a point in space six feet away from your body and imagine the vibrations shooting out of you toward that spot. Call the vibrations back to you.

10 Partially separate from the body.

While keeping your mind entirely focused on what you are doing, increase the vibrational rate in one hand until you feel the hand of the "second body." Raise your astral hand to touch the focus point and push on through.

11 Think about lightness.

Remain focused; let no stray thoughts enter your mind. Deepen your vibrational state. Think how nice it would be to be totally weightless and free.

12 Fully separate from the body.

13 Roam around on the astral plane.

You are now able to observe parts of the world you've never seen before: the spiritual counterparts to physical things and people on Earth as well as ethereal beings and constructs that have no physical manifestation in our universe.

14 Come back.

Close your eyes and focus once again on your physical self, envisioning your presence in it. Your astral self should, after a possibly slow start, snap back to its proper place on the earthly plane.

Be Aware

- It is unlikely but possible that the metaphorical "silver cord," the link between your physical and astral bodies, can be severed while you are projecting. This disruption can be caused by an abrupt trauma to either self and could cause the death of the physical body.
- If you meet other beings on the astral plane, do not have sex with them, since they may be demons.

HOW TO SURVIVE THE BERMUDA TRIANGLE

1 Clean and repair your vessel.

Minimize the risks of traveling in the Bermuda Triangle by performing routine maintenance and a deep systems inspection of your vehicle before setting out on your journey. Many ships lost in the Triangle experienced straightforward mechanical problems, such as malfunctioning radar or a surfeit of benzene residue along the cargo tanks, which can explode when in contact with electrical systems. Test all communication, safety, and backup systems before entering the region.

2 Remain in radio contact at all times.

Beginning 30 minutes before you enter the triangle, maintain radio and electronic communication contact with other ships and contacts on land. Keep these communication lines open for the duration of your travel through the triangle.

3 Compensate for "compass variation."

There is one section of the Bermuda Triangle that is among the rare places on Earth where a compass has been reported to point to the true North Pole, rather than to the Earth's "magnetic north," some 60 miles away, in Canada. Failing to take this difference into account can lead one's navigation astray by as many as 20 degrees. Use a navigational chart that compensates for compass variation, and cross-check your position using multiple compasses as long as you are in the Triangle.

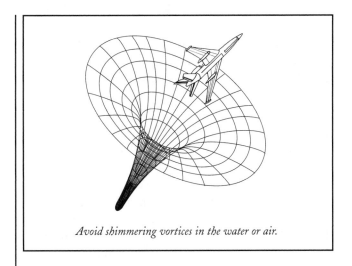

Avoid shimmering vortices in the water or air.

4 Steer around time-space warps.

Some of the missing craft are reported to have been sucked into a tear in the space–time continuum. Watch for a pulsing, brightly illuminated funnel or vortex shimmering in the air or just above the water line. Steer around it.

5 Avoid underwater eruptions.

Other ships are dragged under by eruptions of methane hydrate from the sea floor. Be alert for sudden changes in water temperature, color, and frothiness, which may indicate a reduction in water density sufficient to suck a ship below the surface.

6 Look out for strange fog.

At the first sign of low-hanging gray-green clouds or large patches of mysterious fog, take immediate evasive action. If the electromagnetic fog surrounds your vessel, electric devices, including piloting and navigation systems, will fail.

Be Aware

- The Bermuda Triangle is an approximately 500,000-square-mile swath of the north Atlantic Ocean, wherein an estimated 50 ships and 20 planes have mysteriously disappeared.

- Avoid the Triangle by adjusting your route to take you north of Bermuda (the Triangle's northernmost point); west of Miami, Florida; or south of San Juan, Puerto Rico.

- Theories for the causes of these disappearances vary widely, from electric fields emanating from the ruins of Atlantis to alien life forms living at the ocean's floor to the effect of the Gulf Stream on small unprepared crafts.

- The first person to note the special nature of the Bermuda Triangle was Christopher Columbus, who reported "strange dancing lights on the horizon" as he passed through it in 1492.

- Also known as the Devil's Triangle, the area is only one of the "Vile Vortices," 12 geographic areas spread over the world where frequent paranormal disappearances have been reported. Others include the Devil's Sea Triangle, near Iwo Jima, Japan, and an area southeast of Rio de Janeiro, Brazil.

CHAPTER 4

WITCHES AND WIZARDRY

HOW TO CAST A SPELL

1 Choose the right time and place.

You will need several hours and a space in which total privacy can be assured.

2 Visualize your goal.

Decide exactly what effect you wish to bring about with your spell, such as creating good fortune or financial stability, or having someone fall madly in love with you.

3 Choose your elements.

Decide which spirit it will be appropriate to call upon, depending on your spell's intent. Fire spells involve love and passion; Air spells, thought and communication; Earth spells, stability and healing; Water spells, psychic energy and the subconscious. A spell may call upon any one of the spirits or two or more in combination.

4 Write your spell.

Craft your spell as a series of rhyming couplets. If you can't think of good rhymes, meditate or ask the elemental spirit of Air to help you. Sample couplets include the following: "O strong spirits, ease my strife / and bring sweet peace into my life" and "Spirits below and those above / Grant me friendship, grant me love."

5 Take a ritual bath.

Draw a hot bath, adding to the water one tablespoon of sage and one tablespoon of mugwort. Place an obsidian stone in the tub, light candles around the perimeter, and get in. Remain in the bath for a half hour, calmly meditating on your spell's purpose, to cleanse yourself, in body and spirit, for the sacred task ahead.

6 Don ritual clothing.

Dry off and put on a simple black robe and silver jewelry. Match the jewelry to the spirit you intend to invoke; for example, an amulet depicting a tongue of flame is appropriate for the casting of Fire spells.

7 Put on magical music.

Play recordings of birdsong or chants at a low volume.

8 Cast a magic circle.

Cleanse the room symbolically and literally with a broom, and mark off the edges of a circle with chalk or short lengths of rope. Stand within this space and stare at the edges of the circle until you visualize a shimmering bubble rising up from the edges and surrounding you. This is the magic circle, a space granted you by the spirits in which spell casting has become possible.

9 Chant your spell.

Stand in the center of the circle and slowly chant the spell with eyes closed. Chant the spell at least six times, slowly increasing the speed and volume of recitation, until you feel the power of the spell flowing through you.

10 Return to normal behavior.

Store your ritual items, dress yourself in your everyday clothes, and await the magical adjustment to reveal itself as you have asked.

Be Aware

- Before attempting to solve a problem using a spell, exhaust all nonmagical options. Only when nothing else works will the situation be conducive to magical relief.
- Spells require neither meter nor rhyme, but are more effective if they have them.
- Some witches choose to work "sky clad," meaning naked.
- Record your spell in a magical journal, or "Book of Shadows," for future reference.

SIMPLE SPELL TEMPLATE

Use this simple spell template for quick and effective casting. Choose the elemental power you wish to invoke and customize the objective of the spell as needed.

Oh Spirit of [Earth / Air / Fire / Water], *thou knowest how*
To grant me [objective of spell], *so grant it now!*
In peace and love I call on you
To use your power pure and true
To bring me [objective of spell], *I do implore*
So in your name I ask once more . . .

HOW TO DO
BLACK MAGIC

Black magic, also known as left-handed or Luciferian magic, is spell casting that uses the power of evil to achieve its ends. It is typically employed to bring specific harm to specific people or groups or to call on the power of dark spirits or the Devil to achieve special powers for the spell caster.

⭐ **Choose your victim.**
Most black-magic spells are cast out of malevolent motives, such as to gain revenge on someone who has wronged you or to incapacitate a romantic rival.

⭐ **Wait for a moonlit night.**
The light of the full moon endows black-magic spells with extra power and effectiveness.

⭐ **Steal something from the victim.**
To gain its specific power, a spell requires some corporeal object of significance to the victim, whether a prized possession or personal item such as a lock of hair.

⭐ **Create a magic circle.**
At midnight, enter a dark wood and find a patch of open earth. Using a sharp stick, trace a circle in the dirt and step inside. This magic circle will protect you from the evil spirits you are preparing to call forth.

⭐ **Build a representation of your victim.**
Using tissue paper, wax, buttons, and string, build a small model of the victim; use a black marker to scrawl his or her name along the torso. This effigy need not resemble

the person in any way, as long as you symbolically deem it to be a representation of that specific individual.

⭐ Light a black candle in the center of your circle.
The smoke from a black candle is a strong signal to the dark spirits that you require their presence.

⭐ Ask the dark spirits for assistance.
With eyes closed and hands held over the candle's smoke, explain to the evil spirits why you require their help. Explain how you have been wronged by your intended victim or why you deserve to triumph. Give vent to every petty jealousy and negative impulse.

⭐ Stab the doll.
Plunge knitting needles into the eyes, torso, and limbs of the effigy you built. While stabbing, visualize the fate you have marked out for your victim.

⭐ Set the doll alight.
As it burns, hold your hands over the smoke while imagining the exact fate you intend.

⭐ Let the candle burn all the way down.
Sit cross-legged, with your eyes closed and your mind focused on your hatred. Do not fall asleep.

⭐ Erase the magic circle.
Rise, rub out the magic circle, whisper a final thanks to the dark spirits, and go home. Tell no one what you have done, and remain silent even as the fate you have created for your victim plays out.

Your voodoo doll need not resemble your victim as long as you symbolically note its intended identity.

Be Aware

- Contrary to popular myth, stabbing or burning the doll does not cause stabbing or burning pain to the victim. These are symbolic representations of the desire to do harm.
- Calling on evil spirits for help risks their hanging around and engaging in subsequent mischief in your life.

HOW TO BREW A MAGIC POTION

1 Set an appropriate mood.
Dress in a comfortable robe and light candles. Establish an ongoing rhythm of deep, controlled breaths while meditating upon a mantra—whether "Double, double, toil, and trouble," "Don't stop believing, hold on to the feeling," or anything else that focuses your mental energy upon a rhythmic beat—in order to clear mundane, non-magical thoughts from your mind.

2 Prep your ingredients.
Depending on the ingredients and the recipe, you may need to prepare the component elements of your potion by chopping, dicing, grinding, deboning, blessing, or cursing various items. Prepare these items and arrange them in their correct measure in small bowls close to your cooking area to ensure their smooth combination later.

3 Preheat your cauldron.
Place a 20-quart metal cauldron over an open flame or gas burner set to high. Heat the cauldron until just smoking. Season it with several dashes of the essential oil specified in your recipe. Wait for green smoke to clear before proceeding.

4 Add potion base.
Pour seven quarts of the liquid or liquids that will form the base of your potion, combining water, broths, tinctures, or tears; stir. Reduce heat to simmer.

5 Add ingredients.
Add the remaining wet and dry ingredients, one at a time. Double-check each measurement, for even a small error can result in a drastic change in effect.

6 Walk in a circle.
As you continue to add ingredients and stir, move clockwise with even steps around the cauldron (if heating over an open flame) or in a semicircle at the edge of the stove (if preparing at home).

7 Chant desired effect.
Speak aloud the effect this potion is supposed to have when completed.

8 Stir.
Combine the ingredients by stirring with a long-handled spoon.

9 Cool and serve.

Be Aware
- If no cauldron is available, it is permissible to substitute a cast-iron stockpot of equal volume.
- Many potions call for herbs, which will act more effectively in the potion if the essential oils have been extracted. Soak the herb or root in one or two inches of grapeseed or almond oil in a jar for seven days. Use the resulting herb-infused oil for potion brewing.

Several Useful Potions

 Money tincture.

For the increase of financial health.

- Ingredients: patchouli, clove, nutmeg, cinnamon.
- Rub finished potion on your money before spending it or putting it aside. Within months, you will have more money than in the past.

 Chameleon form.

Grants the ability to change shape and blend in to surroundings.

- Ingredients: rainwater, nectar, green leaves and berries, yellow flowers.
- Brew the night before the full moon; let sit through the next day. Drink one cup before next full moon.

 Love potion.

Causes a person to experience amorous attraction to the potion user.

- Ingredients: lovage, grated lemon peel, oil of orange, oil of lemon, lavender, one piece of lodestone, and one piece of pyrite.
- Place a small dab on your pulse points when near the desired person.

HOW TO TRAIN YOUR FLYING MONKEYS

1 Start early.
Separate the baby monkeys from their mother immediately after birth. Feed the litter by hand and bottle to develop a bond.

2 Teach them your scent.
Give each monkey an old sock or scrap of heraldic robe to play with so that the longing for your scent becomes instinctual.

3 Start with the basics.
Begin with simple, easy-to-master tricks, like sitting up, rolling over, and hovering for a few seconds. Only when a monkey masters these basics should you attempt sustained flying.

4 Demonstrate commands.
Say, "Roll over," and then show them how to roll over. Say, "Fly," and then show them how to fly across the room. Say, "Kill," and get them to violently tear the head off a doll.

5 Repeat.
Be consistent. Drill each monkey for several hours a day, every day.

6 Offer rewards.
Each time the monkey successfully flies across the room, offer a banana. Each time a monkey successfully tears the head off an enemy with its fearsome monkey grip, two bananas.

Laugh evilly as the monkeys fly off to fullfil your worst intentions.

7 Punish.

If they poop on the floor, one rap on the nose with a rolled up-newspaper. If they poop on your head while flying across the room, two raps on the nose.

8 Fit each monkey for a little hat.

Rap them on the nose with the newspaper if they take off their hats.

9 Show them who is boss.

Once the monkeys have mastered the basic commands, capriciously and unpredictably dole out newspaper punishments or banana rewards in such a way that the monkeys are unsure quite what to expect from you. They will then maintain attention and be eager to anticipate and do your bidding.

10 Set them loose to do your evil will.

Throw your head back and cackle evilly as the monkeys fly off to fulfill your worst intentions.

HOW TO CHOOSE AN ANIMAL FAMILIAR

⭐ Listen to your instincts.
Instinctive connection is the single-most important factor in selecting an animal familiar. Think about whether there is a species of animal to which you have always felt a strong connection, such as horse, butterfly, or fish.

⭐ Consider your lifestyle.
Guide or narrow your selection by considering qualities about yourself and compare them to animal behaviors. For instance, are you vegetarian or carnivorous? Are you shy or companionable? Do you prefer to sleep on the ground or in a tree?

⭐ Look past the expected animals.
Do not limit your consideration to animals that match the traditional image of a magical familiar (cats, owls, ravens). A familiar animal can be anything—a goat, a wasp, an inchworm, a tiger, and so on.

⭐ Find a specimen.
Depending on the particular animal you have chosen, it may be easier (dog, cat) or more difficult (white panda) to make contact.

⭐ Clear your mind of impurities.
Before approaching the animal, take deep breaths, fill your mind with positive imagery, and don whatever healing or good-energy amulet you are most comfortable with.

★ Test the psychic connection.
With a clear mind and open heart, keep steady visual contact with the animal, rhythmically murmuring your name and that of the animal, until the two words blend into one. Reach gently for the animal, watchful for an empathetic look or gesture of welcome that will signal psychic connection.

★ If the animal attacks, leave it alone.
Seek a different animal familiar.

Be Aware

- It is also possible, though more difficult, to seek out a familiar on a journey to the astral plane. (See "How to Project Yourself on the Astral Plane," page 140.)
- An animal familiar, once acquired, may serve a family through several generations.
- A "low familiar" is an inanimate object through which you can more singularly focus your magical energies. The most effective of these items will represent power to you: a crystal if you deal in visions, a book if your magic is heavily spell-based, a wand or rod if you regularly stir potions, a mask if you work illusions.
- It is believed by some witches who specialize in black magic that familiars are actually lesser demons or imps in animal shape, and then can be controlled only through a pact with the devil. While a pact with the devil is one option for gaining an animal familiar, it is not the only one.

Frequent Familiars

Familiar	Primary Traits of Mistress
Black Cat	Independence, self-assurance
Fish	Instinctual, in touch with subconscious
Songbird	Lightness of spirit, high intelligence
Frog	Adaptiveness
Hare	Speed, perspicacity
Dog	Protection, truth seeking
Raven	Inquisitive intelligence
Lizard	Healing, spiritual growth
Wolf	Ferocity, power
Insect	Speed, survival instincts
Fox	Cleverness, dexterity
Coyote	Perceptiveness
Spider	Artfulness, preparedness
Rat	Determination, hardiness
Falcon	Discernment, instinct
Owl	Thoughfulness
Viper	Precision, rapidity
Monkey	High intelligence, initiative
Dolphin	Extreme cuteness

HOW TO CURSE SOMEONE

1 Await the new moon.

Cursing in all its forms is more effective when performed under a full moon. It has been suggested that this effectiveness is due to "biological tides": the moon exerting its pull upon a person's bodily fluids, just as it does upon the oceans.

2 Gather objects related to the victim.

Photographs of the person to be cursed, clothing bearing his scent, and objects of special significance are all of value. If other people appear in the photographs, make sure to cut out or digitally erase them before using the photo as part of a curse; failing to do so risks also cursing the others in the picture.

3 Create a magical atmosphere.

Find a quiet, dry, clear space outdoors under the open night sky and draw a circle on the ground. Use chalk or a stick to mark the earth.

4 Focus your energies.

Sit cross-legged in the circle, surrounded by the objects from and images of the individual you wish to curse. Meditate on your feelings about the cursee, inwardly reciting his offenses, while touching and looking at the objects. Focus on these feelings until all other thoughts are banished, leaving you with your negative image of the individual and your intention to curse.

5 | Burn the photographs.
Light a candle and hold a photograph of the cursee over the flame. While it burns, vividly imagine the fate you'd like the person to suffer. In the moment the flame has fully consumed the photograph, speak the words aloud. Repeat until all photographs have been similarly burned.

6 | Funnel cruelty into the objects.
Lift each of the objects of profound meaning to the cursee and stare at it fixedly, repeating the words "I curse you" three times before taking up the next object.

7 | Rise from the sacred space.
Erase the circle.

8 | Inscribe a *tabella defixionum*, or "curse tablet."
On a stone tablet or thin piece of lead, inscribe the name of the cursee, followed by the intended result.

9 | Bury the *tabella defixionum*.
Take the tablet to a graveyard, historic battle site, or other place where the presence of the dead can be felt and bury it there.

10 | Steel yourself.
Pity weakens the power of a curse. As the cursee endures his dire fate, remind yourself of your reasons for laying the curse.

Be Aware

- The *tabellae defixionum* were a fixture of life in ancient Rome, frequently employed to gain personal and professional advantage over rivals.

- A simpler but less reliable cursing method is the "evil eye," in which the curser stares balefully at the cursee, wishing cruelties upon them.

- Your intended cursee may possess a curse-blocking device, such as an amulet, precious stone, or lapis lazuli inscribed with an anticurse spell. These devices can work even if the bearer does not know she is being cursed. Another popular defense is the sign of the horns, in which the index and little fingers are extended while the thumb holds down the middle and ring fingers; although this gesture has become known as one of approval, adopted by heavy-metal rock music fans, its origin is as a repellent to bad luck.

How to Break a Curse

★ Destroy cursed objects.
Recover the items that were used to cast the curse and destroy them. The most effective method is by fire.

★ Bless the cursed objects.
If you are unable or unwilling to burn one of the cursed objects, ask a priest or shaman to utter a blessing over it; depending on the power of the person who laid the curse, this act may have sufficient power to counteract it.

★ Unbury the *tabella defixionum*.
If you know that someone has buried a curse tablet, dig it up and destroy it. Minimize as much as possible the disruption of the graveyard or battle site where the tablet has been buried, since such defilement can earn you a new and more powerful curse.

★ Pray.
Appeal to God or the gods to undo the curse laid upon you. Promise future acts of goodness or behavioral modification.

★ Appeal to the curser.
Apologize for past wrongs and beg her to remove the curse.

★ Lay a vengeance curse.
Cursing the curser in return will not reliably lead to her lifting the curse on you, but it can make you feel better.

CHAPTER 5

FATE, TIME, AND CHANCE

HOW TO MAKE A DEAL WITH DEATH

1 State your proposal upfront.
Let Death know from the outset how much time you'd like and how you'd like to go.

2 Don't accept Death's first offer.
Death is obligated to take a hard line. Don't let yourself be shaken by Death's insistence on a "right here, right now" stance.

3 Make Death a counteroffer.
Find a realistic middle ground between your offer and the one Death proposes. For example, if he says, "Tomorrow, wolves," respond with, "Five years from now, skiing accident."

4 Don't appear too enthusiastic.
Make it seem like continued life isn't that big a deal to you.

5 Keep it professional.
Death will not respond to pleading, crying, or complaining about unfairness. Death has heard it all before.

6 Look Death in the eye.
Or, if Death has come in his traditional guise, look into the black vortex beneath Death's cowl.

7 Ask to speak to Death's supervisor.
Tell him you cannot agree to die without speaking directly to God about the matter.

8 Finalize.
Put the final agreement in writing, and sign in blood.

9 Use the "nibbling" negotiation technique.
At the last possible moment, demand more concessions.
As Death reaches forward to sign the contract, say, "Oh,
this does include reincarnation, right?"

How to Beat Death at Chess

⭐ Distract Death.
Point over Death's shoulder and ask, "Hey, is that Elvis?"
When he looks, quickly and quietly move one of your
pieces to a more advantageous position.

⭐ Question Death.
Ask Death if he's *sure* that's his next move. If he says yes,
raise your eyebrows and say, "OK, that's cool." If Death
then says, "Wait, hold on a second," sigh heavily and say,
"Fine."

⭐ Go to the bathroom.
While in the restroom, consult a strategy book or minia-
ture board.

⭐ Use accomplices.
Many people hold a grudge against Death and may be
enlisted to distract him or surreptitiously feed you moves.

⭐ Demand a rematch.
Complain loudly about every aspect of the game. Appeal
to Death's vanity by saying, "If you really want to win that
way, fine. Whatever. Kill me."

⭐ Ask to play Scrabble instead.
Death is terrible at Scrabble.

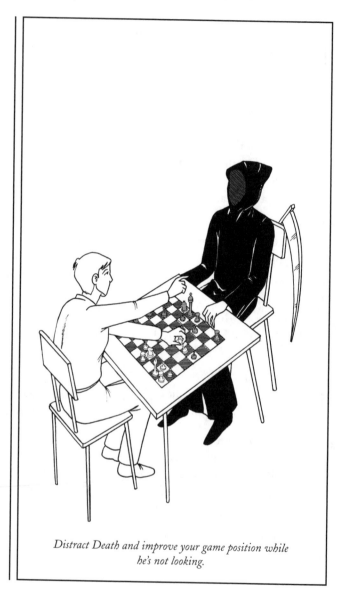

Distract Death and improve your game position while he's not looking.

HOW TO SURVIVE BEING A SURVIVOR OF AN ACCIDENT IN WHICH YOU WERE MEANT TO DIE

⭐ Avoid public transportation.
Do not ride or go near buses, trains, shuttles, trams, trolleys, pedicabs, or horse-drawn carriages.

⭐ Avoid private transportation.
Do not ride or go near cars, vans, trucks, minivans, bicycles, tricycles, motorcycles, or motorcycle sidecars.

⭐ Take baths.
Do not take showers. Before running the water for your bath, unplug all electric devices and lock the bathroom door; while running the water, check the temperature constantly. Stay in the bath only long enough to clean yourself and never more than four minutes.

⭐ Avoid gigantic neon signs.

⭐ Do not swim.
Don't go in the ocean, do laps at the gym, or go to your friend's backyard pool, especially if it is equipped with a suctioning drain.

⭐ Do not go near guns.
Avoid pistols, rifles, handguns, shotguns, BB guns, and nail guns.

✪ Avoid rickety fire-escape ladders.

✪ Avoid trucks with cherry pickers.

✪ Avoid fire.
Do not touch matches, gasoline, downed electric cables, ovens, stoves, or torches. Do not smoke, and do not be friends with or go near people who smoke.

✪ Do not walk by rickety scaffolding.

✪ Do not attempt to rescue other people from death.

✪ Do not go near chain-link fencing.
Be wary of large objects, such as carbon dioxide tanks, that can smash your body into the fencing, thereby dicing it into small pieces.

✪ Do not take elevators.

✪ Do not ride roller coasters.

✪ Do not go near horses.
In fact, avoid animals of all kinds.

Be Aware

The only way to permanently remove Death's attention, after you have survived an accident in which you were meant to die, is to purposefully put yourself in a near-fatal situation and then survive.

HOW TO SURVIVE VIEWING A CURSED JAPANESE VIDEOTAPE

1 Ignore the phone.
Immediately after the tape ends, the phone will ring. If you answer it, a voice will say, "Seven days," and the countdown to your death will begin.

2 Keep the film hidden.
If they find it, your friends and family members will be supernaturally compelled to watch the videotape as well.

3 Identify the people seen in the film.
Look for clues to their identities, such as distinctive clothing, identifying marks, and street addresses glimpsed in the background.

4 Focus on the video's overscan area.
Bring the video to a media postproduction facility and watch it frame by frame, noting any details that appear on the outer edges of the image, which are often invisible on home televisions.

5 Track down the people glimpsed in the movie.
Discover the hidden, horrifying secrets of their pasts, including the story of the child whose premature death and burial resulted in the cursed video. Be firm in your questioning but sensitive to the possibility that your questions may drive the people to suicidal insanity.

6 Dig up the past.

Follow the trail of clues to the body of the child and dig her up.

7 Give the child a proper burial.

Some Japanese ghost-videotape curses are lifted when the disturbed spirit is given a proper burial. Many vengeful ghosts, however, insist that the curse must be passed on to a new victim.

8 Make a copy of the tape.

Hook two VCRs together and copy the image to a second tape.

9 Mail the tape to a randomly selected address.

Pray for forgiveness.

Be Aware

With the advent of new technologies, such as DVD and Blu-ray, a significant problem faced by cursees looking to pass along the videotape may be less about whom to curse than about who has a functioning VCR.

How to Predict the Future

Method	Necessary Equipment	Basic Operation
Scrying	Crystal or glass ball	Gaze into the ball, read the images appearing in the smoky glass
Tasseomancy	Loose tea, wide-brimmed teacup	Swirl leaves clockwise, interpret shapes in jumbled leaves
Haruspicy	Sacrificial animals (especially sheep or poultry), knife	Ritually slaughter the animal, interpret the shapes of its entrails and internal organs
Spatilomancy	Well-fed animal	Peer into the animal's feces, interpret the shapes
Geomancy	Clods of earth or clay	Toss soil on the ground, look for 16 specific geometric patterns
Rhabdomancy	Divining rod	Set rod on end, observe and interpret direction it falls
Oneiromancy	Sleep that results in dreams	Write down dream, interpret based on ancient texts or Freudian theory
Chresmomancy	A mentally unstable person	Listen to lunatic's ravings, heed coded warnings
Ouija board	Decorated wooden game board	Collective subconscious guides hands to spell messages
Tarot	Deck of symbolically decorated cards	Draw from deck and arrange four cards in diamond shape, interpret to answer specific question
Palmistry	Subject's hand	Read the lines, breaks, and furrows of the palm
Astrology	Astrological chart	Cross-reference subject's date and time of birth with current location of celestial bodies
I Ching	Six coins, a copy of the *I Ching* or *Book of Changes*	Flip the coin 6 times and use the head/tail combination to write a hexagram; find it among the 64 interpretable hexagrams of the I Ching
Magic Eight Ball	Oversized billiard ball filled with fluid, magic	Ask questions, shake ball, get answers

HOW TO CONVINCE ANCIENT PEOPLE YOU ARE A GOD

1 Display your finery.

Depending on how ancient the people are that you are visiting, they may possibly be naked; draped in animal furs; clad in simple robes, togas, or tunics; or wearing other simple, hand-crafted garments. Amaze them with your array of synthetic, machine-stitched, and machine-dyed fabrics, revealing each piece of clothing in turn to maximize dramatic effect.

2 Stand up straight.

Even an average-sized contemporary person will tower over ancient people. Draw yourself up to full height, and hold your arms above your head.

3 Show your fillings.

Open your mouth wide to display any gold or silver fillings or caps, which ancient people will understand to be a mark of godhood.

4 Give the ancient people a sip of soda.

Fructose-sweetened carbonated beverages are like nothing that existed in ancient times and can convincingly be explained as divine nectar.

5 Show them your flashlight.

Turn the light on and off quickly to create a strobe effect. Swing the light in a wide arc. Shine it directly into people's eyes.

Share the sweet carbonation of a soda and the musical "magic"
of a cell phone to inspire awe in primitive humans.

6 | Play music on your phone.
Pass the earbuds to each person as you explain that your divine force will speak directly into their souls.

7 | Summon fire from the heavens.
Make a pile of kindling. Then spin a long, thin stick between your hands over an indentation on a flat piece of wood; add dry leaves and blow softly on the resulting spark to create fire. Place the fire amid the kindling. (Note that this will be more impressive the further back you have travelled past the early Stone Age.)

8 | Shock them with electricity.
Vigorously rub your hands on the fabric of your shirt or pants for 30 seconds and then touch the bare arm of an ancient person, causing a static electric shock to jump from your hands to their flesh. When they flinch, say "Pow!"

9 | Predict a celestial event.
Using an almanac or previous knowledge of past events, predict a meteor shower, eclipse, volcanic eruption, or other meteorological incident.

10 | Show them your time machine.
Reveal whatever time- and space-bending machinery you used to travel to the ancient world in the first place. Engage it to send one or more ancient people on quick round-trip visits to the contemporary or future world.

Be Aware

In many ancient societies, a fine line separated "god" and "demon." A single inauspicious event attributed to you, rightly or wrongly, could mark you as a figure to be feared or hated, or as a candidate for human sacrifice. Keep your time machine on standby in case of such a backlash.

HOW TO CONVINCE PRE-INDUSTRIAL PEOPLE YOU ARE NOT A WITCH OR DEMON

1 Hide industrial and post-industrial accoutrements.
Once you have emerged from your time machine or pulsating rend in the time-space continuum, divest yourself of all electronic devices, machine-made tools, and synthetic fabrics. Such items will be unfamiliar and frightening to pre-industrial people. Also remove glasses, jewelry, and shoes.

2 Undo body modifications.
Take out nose rings, earrings, and piercings. Cover tattoos with outergarments or bandages.

3 Move slowly.
Approach the villagers or tribesmen carefully, step by step, using slow and predictable motions. Keep your facial expression neutral and keep your hands held open and loose at your sides.

4 Speak slowly.
Speak in short, simple sentences, using one-syllable words. If it becomes clear that the pre-industrial people do not understand anything, remain silent and communicate with hand gestures alone.

5 | Do not exhibit any of the signs of being a witch.
Do not have three nipples; float if thrown in the water; own a black cat; talk to animals; have a mole, wart, or pimple; be a widow; or fly.

6 | Speak the name of God.
In traditional pre-industrial belief systems, witches and demons are incapable of uttering the name of God. Notice by context what divine power the pre-industrial people are invoking to protect them from you, and repeat that name back to them.

7 | Make the symbol of the cross.
It is believed in Christian cultures that witches and demons cannot bear to see or to make the sign of the cross. If the villagers are making the sign of the cross, do so in return. Do not make the sign of the cross if they have not already done so, or the gesture may be misunderstood.

8 | Aid in local activities.
Show your benevolent intentions by taking part in the life of the hamlet or farming community.

Be Aware

As you integrate into the community, the villagers may think you are an invalid based on the slow speed of your threshing or the poor quality of your loom work.

HOW TO AVOID PARADOXES WHILE TIME TRAVELING

1 Obey the Butterfly Principle.
Injure no living thing, no matter how small, to avoid an unforeseen chain of events that will permanently alter the present (i.e., the past's future).

2 Obey the Hitler Maxim.
Do not kill or injure any human being in any way, even if your future knowledge suggests it would be beneficial to all humankind. If you change history in a substantial fashion, you may find it impossible to return to anything resembling the life you once knew.

3 Do as the Romans do.
Hew as closely as possible to period-appropriate modes of dress and conduct.

4 Don't bet.
Avoid the temptation to use your knowledge of future events to make money in the stock market or lottery, or betting on sporting events.

5 Don't introduce technologies.
Do not employ any technologies antedating the time period you are visiting; when traveling forward in time, do not use any technologies you do not understand.

6 Keep to yourself.
Do not form friendships. Do not interfere with existing friendships or counsel anyone to either form or end a romantic attachment.

Avoid becoming involved with your parents'
younger selves while time traveling.

7 Keep your hands to yourself.
Do not make love to, flirt with, or in any way become romantically involved with anyone.

8 Stay away from yourself.
Make no attempt to communicate with, warn, or threaten younger versions of yourself.

9 Stay away from your parents.
Make no attempt to communicate with, warn, or threaten younger versions of your own parents.

10 Stay away from your grandparents.
Etc., etc., etc.

11 Go home.
Limit your stay in a given period to no more than one hour. The longer you stay in the past, the greater the risk that your actions may create a paradox.

12 Go home empty-handed.
Do not bring home souvenirs of the past. Do not invite ancient philosophers, conquerors, or cowboys to appear as visual aids in a school project.

13 Return if necessary.
If, on arriving home, you are confronted with major differences in the present day that are clearly traceable to specific actions you took in the past, go back and stop yourself from performing those actions. Do not injure or kill yourself in doing so.

HOW TO TELL IF YOU'RE IN THE TWILIGHT ZONE

Any of the following warning signs may indicate that you have entered this nebulous, existential state of being.

⭐ **Sudden advent of narration.**
Listen for a menacing voiceover making cryptic, insinuating suggestions about you or your future.

⭐ **Aggressive normalcy of environment.**
Look for signs that everything in your life, marriage, small Midwestern town, or home planet is absolutely typical, indicating a high chance that this will all soon be upended.

⭐ **Singularity of unusualness.**
Be on the alert for one significantly unusual trait in an otherwise normal home, newly met stranger, or talking doll.

⭐ **Something only you can see.**
If you encounter a creepy old man, talking object, or gremlin hunched on the wing of an airplane, obtain corroboration from another person that the old man, object, or gremlin is not a hallucination or haunting.

⭐ **Dreams coming true.**
If you have suddenly achieved everything you've ever desired, be on the lookout for an unexpected but devastating turn of events.

★ Alien invasion.
The Twilight Zone is heavily populated by alien life forms, ranging from the evil to the seemingly benign but in reality still evil.

★ Survival of an accident that should have killed you.
See also How to Tell If You're Dead (p. 39) and How to Survive Being a Survivor of an Accident in Which You Were Meant to Die (p. 173).

★ Car trouble.
Inexplicable engine breakdown is a frequent sign of Twilight Zone entry, especially if the car failure leaves the driver and passengers stranded in a diner or occurs when a hitchhiker is present.

★ Signs of anachronicity.
Watch for events or locations that seem to belong to another time, such as a commuter train that stops in the late 1800s.

★ Your town is ruled by a cruel and omniscient teenage boy.

Be Aware

- The very nature of the Twilight Zone suggests that it is often impossible to tell that you have entered the Twilight Zone.
- As a general rule, escape from the Twilight Zone is achieved only through death or by embracing the bitter irony of life.
- If the narration announces that it will "control the horizontal and the vertical," you are in the Outer Limits.
- If you find the strange events unfolding around you revealed in a disturbing oil painting, you are in the Night Gallery.

ABOUT THE AUTHORS

David Borgenicht is the creator and coauthor of all the books in the *Worst-Case Scenario* series, and is president and publisher of Quirk Books (www.quirkbooks.com). He is a big fan of zombies, magic, and Star Trek. He lives in Philadelphia.

Ben H. Winters is the coauthor of *Sense and Sensibility and Sea Monsters*, *Android Karenina*, and *The Worst-Case Scenario Pocket Guides* for *Cars*, *Cats*, *Meetings*, *New York City*, and *San Francisco*.

Brenda Brown is an illustrator and cartoonist whose work has been published in many books and publications, including the *Worst-Case Scenario* series, *Esquire*, *Reader's Digest*, *USA Weekend*, *21st Century Science & Technology*, the *Saturday Evening Post*, and the *National Enquirer*. Her website is www.webtoon.com.

THE FIRST OF THE WORST

The
WORST-CASE SCENARIO
Survival Handbook

HOW TO:
→ Escape from Quicksand
→ Wrestle an Alligator
→ Break Down a Door
→ Land a Plane …

By Joshua Piven and David Borgenicht

⚠ 3 million copies
in print

⚠ Translated into
27 languages

⚠ International
bestseller

"An armchair guide for
the anxious."
—*USA Today*

"The book to have when the
killer bees arrive."
—*The New Yorker*

"Nearly 180 pages of immediate
action drills for when everything
goes to hell in a handbasket."
—*Soldier of Fortune*

"This is a really nifty book."
—*Forbes*

A BOOK FOR EVERY DISASTER

Also Available in Digital Editions

HANDBOOKS

Original

Travel

Dating & Sex

Golf

Holidays

Work

College

Weddings

Parenting

Extreme Edition

Life

Paranormal

Almanacs

History

Great Outdoors

Politics

Pocket Guides

Dogs

Cats

New York City

San Francisco

Retirement

Breakups

Meetings

Cars

Also Available

- *The Complete Worst-Case Scenario Survival Handbook*
- *The Complete Worst-Case Scenario Survival Handbook: Man Skills*
- *The Worst-Case Scenario Book of Survival Questions*
- *The Worst-Case Scenario Daily Survival Calendar*